D1196928

EFFECTIVE LIBRARY EXHIBITS

HOW TO PREPARE AND PROMOTE GOOD DISPLAYS

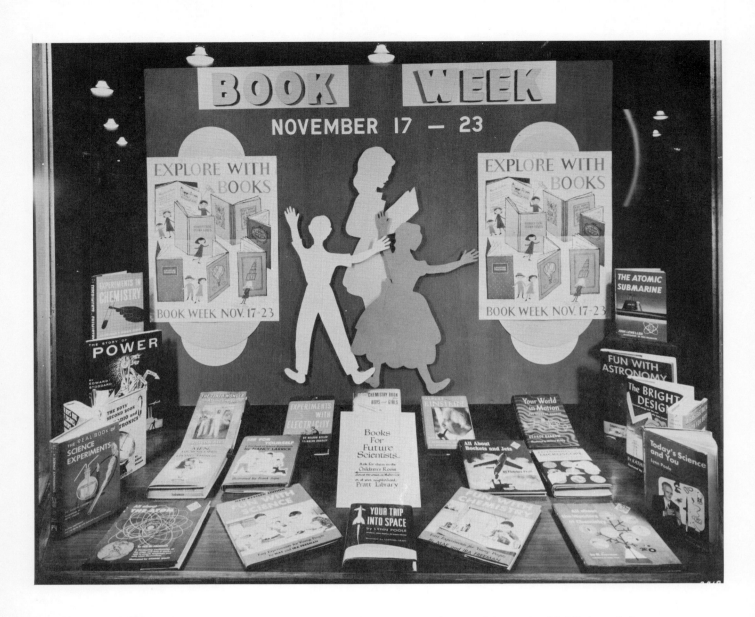

SIMPLICITY IN DESIGN *Vari-sized cardboard circles emphasizing color highlights of the posters, serve as added decoration and help point up the display theme.*

EFFECTIVE LIBRARY EXHIBITS

HOW TO PREPARE AND PROMOTE GOOD DISPLAYS

By Kate Coplan

Chief, Exhibits and Publicity, Enoch Pratt Free Library

Introduction by Gerald W. Johnson

OCEANA PUBLICATIONS • NEW YORK

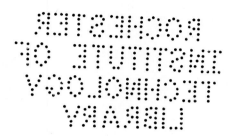

Printed in the United States of America
by Oceana Publications, Inc., New York, N. Y.

CONTENTS

CONTENTS (continued)

ILLUSTRATIONS

TO

FOUR CHAMPIONS OF LIBRARY EXHIBITS

JOSEPH L. WHEELER
(*Who gave me opportunity and guidance*)

EMERSON GREENAWAY

and

AMY WINSLOW
(*Who supported and encouraged me*)

ARTHUR H. PARSONS, JR.
(*Without whose stimulating interest this book
would not have been written*)

— K. C.

If you are in Baltimore, and you wish to know what is going on in the city other than accidents, fires, crimes and equally unpredictable sensations, you have only to take a stroll of one city block on Cathedral Street between Franklin and Mulberry. That block is occupied by the Enoch Pratt Free Library's central building, with twelve show windows, like those of a department store, each window telling a story of something that is occupying the attention of some of the people of Baltimore during the current period.

Is some national fraternity, or trade association, or learned society holding its annual convention in the city? A window will be devoted to the organization, mentioning the meeting and displaying a book — more likely thirty books — on its history and its work. Has a Baltimore author just published a new book? That book will be there, with a bulletin describing it. Is it the anniversary of some historic event? There will be pictures, books, relics of all kinds, relating to the event. Is some other cultural institution — university, college, conservatory, museum, art institute, putting on a special show of some kind? The library will publicize it, and will ransack its own shelves for material bearing on the subject.

In short, here is a visual display of the intellectual life of the city during the three weeks covered. The passer-by with a special interest in one of the subjects has only to step inside the building to find further information and a skillfully assembled collection of printed material relating to it.

The object of this program is first to stimulate and then to satisfy the intellectual curiosity of the Baltimore public, which is, of course, the function of any public library. Evidence of its effectiveness in that regard is the enormous increase in circulation since the system was adopted. But it has had another effect, not so easily measurable, but very great and valuable.

This effect is the integration of the institution with the life of the city ouside its walls. The individual passing along that block may not see in the windows anything of strong and direct interest to him, anything that causes him to pause and study a particular exhibit; but he cannot fail to gain the impression that the library is alive and alert, interested in whatever the citizens of Baltimore are doing, and ready to extend its good offices to help the work along. So when something comes along that does interest him, his steps turn in that direction to see what the library has made of it; and he is usually pleased.

This is one of the strong factors contributing to the vitality of the institution. Time was when the Pratt, like too many other public libraries, was regarded by the public as pretty much a mausoleum of dead ideas, but that was long ago. Today the place is as alive as the post office, and rather more alive than the City Hall. Quiet is enforced in the reading rooms and you can study there very comfortably. But the Pratt is no place for meditation; there is too much going on, and things go on because the people have been made aware of the services that are available in the library.

The idea of assimilating the library into the main current of the city's economic and cultural life was the brain-child of Joseph L. Wheeler, a great librarian; but it has been carefully fostered by Mr. Wheeler's successors in the years since his retirement, and today is going stronger than ever. It is doubtful that there is another big-city library in the country that touches the life of its town more intimately at more points, and this program of salesmanship — for that is what it is — is one of the most important factors in the establishment and maintenance of those contacts.

It is proof of Wheeler's genius that he never did what was expected, but he rarely did anything more surprising than when he entrusted his visual display program to a staff member then a mere slip of a girl. But it was one of his shrewdest appointments. Kate Coplan had no experience in 1927, but she had energy, imagination and, above all, the capacity to learn from her own mistakes, that is to say, the capacity of growth. Through the years, and in the rough but effective school of trial and error, she has matured into a woman who knows as much about this phase of library work as anyone in the United States — some able librarians from other cities have told me that she knows more.

This volume is a distillation of the wisdom that she has been gathering for thirty years. Whether or not it is a contribution to library science I am not competent to decide; but I know beyond peradventure that it is a contribution to library operation, assuming that one aspiration of the library is to be, not a mere adjunct, but a vital, indispensable part of the society to which it belongs.

Nevertheless, it omits one tremendously important step in the creation of a really fine program of visual display, and for the benefit of librarians who consult the volume, and without anybody's permission, I herewith supply that omission. As in the old recipe for rabbit stew, the first direction reads, "first catch your rabbit," so to anyone who envisages a program that shall outshine that of the Enoch Pratt Free Library of Baltimore, I offer this counsel: first catch your Kate Coplan.

— *Gerald W. Johnson*

Baltimore
August, 1958

ACKNOWLEDGMENTS

In the preparation of this book, the author has had much valuable assistance. Special thanks are due Mr. Lee Ash and Mrs. Sylvia Auerbach, editor and managing editor, respectively, of the *Library Journal,* for permission to use excerpts from that publication; Mr. Alfred I. Zipprian and Mr. G. Wilson Younglove, of the Baltimore Gas and Electric Company, for help with the chapter on Lighting; William and Elliott Becker, Baltimore display specialists, for a number of useful ideas; Miss Sara I. Fenwick, editor, for permission to quote from *Top of the News,* published by the Young Adult Services Division and the Children's Services Division of the American Library Association, and Mr. Lynn Poole, director of public relations at the Johns Hopkins University, for cooperation on the list of sources of free display materials.

Further, the author is particularly indebted to the following persons and groups associated with her "Alma Mater," the Enoch Pratt Free Library: Arthur H. Parsons, Jr., director, for reading the manuscript and making many constructive suggestions; the Board of Trustees, for official approval of the project; Mrs. Margaret A. Edwards, coordinator of work with young adults, for aid with the Book Fair notes; Mrs. Freda Freyer, children's librarian at the Edmondson Avenue Branch, for information presented in Tips to Teachers; Mr. Stewart Duncan, of the Business Office, for contributing to the compilation of data concerning sources of display supplies; Mr. Charles Cipolloni, of the Exhibits and Publicity Division, for spade work in connection with the Basic Silk Screen section, and to other members of the Exhibits staff — Mrs. Constance Rosenthal, Mrs. Lorraine Stonesifer, Mr. Frank Cipolloni and Mr. Ronald Hess — for various tasks cheerfully performed. The majority of the photographs are by Mr. Edgar Schaefer, Mr. Sidney Sussman and Mr. William Ochs.

— *Kate Coplan*

Baltimore, Maryland
August, 1958

EFFECTIVE LIBRARY EXHIBITS

HOW TO PREPARE AND PROMOTE GOOD DISPLAYS

CHAPTER ONE

THE CASE FOR EXHIBITS

The modern world has traveled far since the days when people had to depend on lay minstrels, journeying at a snail's pace from village to village, for word-of-mouth news and information.

Today, through a network of libraries, books and information are available for the asking in almost every quarter of the globe. Yet all too few people realize how their everyday lives can be affected and improved by the vast wealth of knowledge which has been accumulated through the centuries and awaits them in books on the shelves of their libraries.

No library, regardless of its size, complexion or financial status, can afford to overlook exhibits as a means of widening its sphere of influence and service. Not only public libraries, but also school and college libraries, industrial libraries, special libraries — all have an opportunity through exhibits to make their readers, present and potential, more aware of their resources and facilities.

Library materials that simply sit on the shelves are just so much dead wood, the money, time and labor expended on their acquisition and processing largely wasted. Through dra-

READING REMINDERS

Although libraries have on their shelves books and information relating to many diversified subjects, only a small percentage of the people in their communities know and draw on the collections. Through eye-catching displays the availability of the various types of printed materials can be emphasized repeatedly, thereby stimulating their use.

Visual presentation has gained continual momentum in recent years. Virtually every field of endeavor — business, industry, agriculture, science, education, even the social services — has stepped up its use of display to interpret its aims and achievements to the public. Certainly libraries, which have so much to offer in the field of education and recreation, cannot lag behind.

matic displays many of these inactive items can be restored to life, thereby fulfilling the authors', publishers' and librarians' intent.

Worthwhile exhibits intelligently presented and enthusiastically promoted, build up an amazing reservoir of good will. They need not cost much, but any investment of funds and staff effort is bound to pay off handsomely in greater usefulness of the materials displayed, and beyond that, in improved public relations and added prestige for the library. Indirectly thereby the library's budget is favorably affected.

I should like to emphasize here that attractive, meaningful exhibits can be produced at relatively low cost. If no separate budget is available for the purpose, there is always the petty cash drawer to fall back on. With ingenuity and resourcefulness, with taste and discrimination, library workers can accomplish creditable displays with minimum outlay.

Many commercial display pieces, their advertising matter judiciously deleted, adapt well to library exhibitions. I remember, years ago, begging an attractive whiskey display that I saw mounted in a tavern window. It featured a high-stepping majorette with baton in hand,

and when the cardboard frame bearing the advertising copy was removed, it made a colorful backdrop decoration for a window display on music.

Baseball figurines from a brewery ad; basketball players from a cigarette ad; oversize paper strawberries from an ice cream manufacturer; tempting food pictures fom a delicatessen — these are some of the items obtained free of charge from Baltimore commercial establishments and adapted for library display purposes.

When we undertook our exhibits program at the Enoch Pratt Free Library back in 1927, we started on the proverbial shoestring. There was no budget, no staff, not even adequate work space.

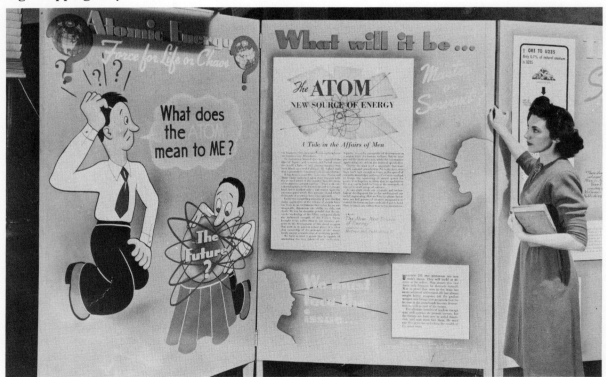

WIDENING HORIZONS   *While history plays its inevitable part in display programs, the library also has a responsibility to keep readers informed of important current and possible future ideas, discoveries and developments. When atomic energy was "new" the Enoch Pratt Free Library arranged a comprehensive exhibition — in cooperation with the Maryland Academy of Sciences — of which these were the introductory panels.*

22

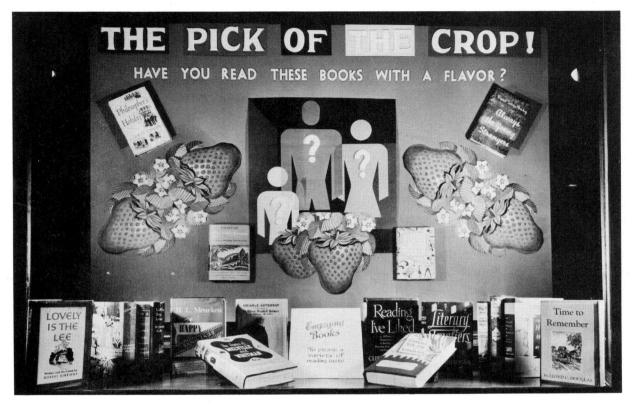

THE PICK OF THE CROP!

HAVE YOU READ THESE BOOKS WITH A FLAVOR?

FREE MATERIALS *Many attractive pieces which adapt well to display design may be had free for the asking. In the accompanying illustration are a poster originally issued to advertise the high rate of tuberculosis, and oversize paper strawberries supplied by the Hendler Creamery Company, Baltimore.*

My "office" at the time consisted of a small typewriter table set between two large iron stacks in the old reference room. For fixtures I had the maintenance man build a few small pedestals and tables from odds and ends of lumber lying in the basement. Pieces of discarded wallboard, and cardboard cartons, when covered with gay paper or cheap cloth, served as backdrops and book stands.

Because we had no good areas of our own suitable for displays, Mr. Joseph L. Wheeler, then director, suggested that I borrow vacant store windows in the busy downtown district, to show library materials. After several frustrating attempts, some real estate representatives finally agreed to the temporary loan of a few windows for library displays, provided the FOR RENT signs remained conspicuously placed. (Later, when the rental agents discovered that the exhibits helped lease their properties more quickly, they eagerly sought additional displays.)

A 73-year-old porter on the staff was assigned as my part-time helper. We had no truck or car in those days, and I can picture us still as we walked down the street. On one arm the porter carried a slat basket of books. On the other arm he had a pail and cleaning equipment, for almost invariably the glass of the borrowed windows was so dirty that it was difficult to see through. We always had to beg a bucket of water from the corner drugstore to get the glass washed before each exhibit was installed.

In a position without precedent, one learns by doing. Without proper funds or resources one must improvise, borrow, adapt, stretch whatever is available so it will do double or triple duty. In those early days, to our great surprise and delight — with everything in a given display borrowed except the sign calling attention to the fact that the books were obtainable at the Pratt Library — we won second prize in a national window display contest.

Here in this instance is proof that libraries with even the most limited of funds can embark on a successful exhibits program. Little by little equipment, letter stocks, decorations, will build up until the supply is in satisfactory working order.

One point, however, must be made crystal clear. Library exhibits, to be successful, must be well planned, organized and executed. Amateurish, "home-made" looking displays — whether window displays, bulletin board displays, panel displays, case, table or shelf displays — should be avoided like the plague. Poor lettering, clashing colors, bad art, inexpert arrangement are a discredit, rather than a credit to the library.

Workers without formal art training or natural talent would do well, whenever possible, to enlist the abilities of others. If they can obtain the assistance of advertising specialists, artists or students with a flair for display, the results are likely to be gratifying for both the library and the participants.

Competent students in art classes may contribute posters, show cards and other items for effective exhibits. Vocational classes, and individuals handy with tools, will be glad to turn out small book fixtures and additional pieces of equipment if the "makings" are supplied by the library. In Baltimore we remember with gratitude the early help given by vocational units in the public schools, and by the Maryland Institute.

Few library activities bring the rich rewards that displays do. If they are interesting enough and attractive enough and frequent enough, they can turn many indifferent viewers into active, enthusiastic library users and supporters.

FRUITFUL COOPERATION *Good posters and other display items may be obtained without cost to the library if artists, art students and teachers are invited to cooperate. These posters were among those made as a class project years ago for the Enoch Pratt Free Library, by students of the Maryland Institute.*

CHAPTER TWO

DISPLAY IDEAS AND ARRANGEMENT

This is the age of visual education, and libraries must make the most of that fact. Today the most successful agencies everywhere are those which tell the world by every feasible means — especially pictorial presentation — who they are, where they are, what they are doing, why they are doing it and how they are doing it. If the library is to serve as a truly constructive force in the community, then it must make more people aware of how the printed word can help them in their homes, in their jobs, with their educational and recreational problems.

The purpose of library exhibits, of course, is to stimulate interest in books and reading, and to show how the library's services and resources can aid individuals and groups in the community. In the course of a single year a library can place before the public a comprehensive cross-section of its collection, demonstrating how books and other materials tie in with the community's interests.

To the general viewer, a display represents a sampling of what the library has to offer him. All too frequently one observes exhibits distinguished only for lack of novelty, poor art and lettering, or uninteresting design. A display is a good deal like an individual. To be a success in life it must be friendly and appealing, it must have color, balance, personality, and even a sense of humor on occasion. It must please before it can inform. Any exhibit lacking these qualities is likely to fail.

Displays may be devoted to science, art, industry, agriculture, health, literature, business, labor, education, civic and social problems, with emphasis on local achievements in these fields. National and international events, birthdays and deaths of notables, seasonal topics, holidays, commemorative occasions, these are all grist for the display mill. In addition, opportunity is given for the showing of handicraft

DISPLAY IDEAS FOR THE NEW YEAR

Early in January people seem more receptive to suggestions of self-improvement. The "readers" were raised on insulite blocks, to give a three-dimensional quality.

and hobby collections, travelling exhibitions and items from fine private libraries.

Since the displays are to be viewed by persons of all ages, interests and walks of life, the material must be varied in scope and reading level. As in all library activities, an effort should be made to present various points of view, particularly on questions about which there are widely supported, differing shades of public opinion.

Bulletin boards, exhibition cases, free-standing panels, shelves and tables within the library become excellent channels for conveying whatever information the library desires to present. But exterior show windows are far more important, because the chief aim is to carry the reading message to persons not already familiar with the library's facilities and potential usefulness.

UPCOMING HOLIDAYS *Can tie in with a variety of books worthy of display.*

For this purpose well-located window space is essential. A display buried on a side street where there is little pedestrian or motor traffic, is just so much waste of time, effort and energy.

Perhaps the leading grocer on the main street will lend his window for a week or two. As this will represent some sacrifice on his part, the librarian can show appreciation by displaying some tempting cook books, thus promoting not only the books, but also the grocer's wares.

In the spring a hardware merchant might be induced to give up a show window temporarily to an exhibition of garden literature. He will consent with alacrity if a collection of his garden implements can be included in the design. When properly approached almost any shop owner, as a matter of self-interest, will be happy to fall in line with the library's plan.

One almost infallible method for producing a popular exhibit is to include objects lent by some member or members of the immediate community. If 10-year-old Johnny, for example, has built a detailed model of a jet plane, or a teen-age girl has woven a gay rug from old stockings, and you feature these in a handicraft display, success is virtually assured. Not only will the youngsters and their friends make visits to gaze and admire, but so will the doting sisters, brothers, uncles and aunts, not to mention the proud parents.

Also, there is nothing like word-of-mouth advertising. And when Mrs. Smith, oh, so casually, mentions to Mrs. Jones that her Mary is having a rug exhibited by the library, Mrs. Jones will hardly fail to stop by for a look on her way to market.

Ideas for exhibits need not necessarily be

26

original. Any alert librarian can discover a wealth of suggestions in books, newspapers and magazines, on book jackets, in advertising and publicity journals. A casual walk down the street may yield a number of effective ideas to workers with a seeing eye and a bit of imagination. For instance, a man observed wrestling with the problem of a stalled car at a busy intersection might suggest a display on the care and repair of automobiles. The sight of two corpulent matrons sipping frothy sodas in a drug store might prompt consideration of a display featuring diet and nutrition.

As has been said before, artists and art students, teachers in the community, hobbyists and collectors often may be persuaded to contribute ideas, time and material. The more the librarian can get others to do, the less he will have to do himself. Usually ready and willing allies in exhibits undertakings are the public schools.

At the Enoch Pratt Free Library special attention is paid to significant books written by authors presently residing in Baltimore or elsewhere in Maryland. To give recognition and encouragement to local writing talent, the library frequently devotes an entire window exhibit to a single new volume of widespread public interest. Thirty copies of the work are borrowed from the publisher, along with original art, if any, and a photograph of the author, to add a personal touch.

STORE — LIBRARY COOPERATION *A window display in Baltimore's well-known, century-old department store, HUTZLER BROTHERS CO., featuring gardening books from the public library, along with related implements from the store's garden shop. On the back "fence" was posted the following sign: "Whatever your hobby, your job, your research, your travel plans . . . You'll find just the Books to give you 'a lift' at the Enoch Pratt Free Library. Trained librarians are ready to help you."*

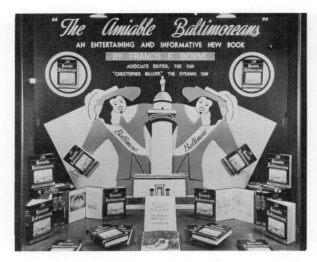

"ASSIST" FOR LOCAL AUTHORS *Through its window displays the Enoch Pratt Free Library gives recognition to significant books by writers presently residing in Baltimore or elsewhere in Maryland.*

Often ready-made exhibits are available for borrowing, with a minimum of effort and labor on the part of the library. Among sources for such displays are schools and colleges, art and science museums, government bureaus, industries, labor unions, transportation and travel agencies. All borrowed materials should be insured against fire, theft and damage, both in transit and while in the library's possession.

In Baltimore it has long been the practice to provide small library exhibits for worthwhile "outside" programs. To name but a few to which the Pratt has sent book displays: child care and training centers; church conferences; United Nations activities; a leadership forum conducted by the Junior Association of Commerce; family affairs institutes and film forums.

EXAMPLE OF A BORROWED DISPLAY

For its second Atomic Energy Institute the Enoch Pratt Free Library borrowed from the American Museum of Atomic Energy at Oak Ridge, Tenn., a fine show, professionally prepared. Shipped to Baltimore in specially-designed crates, the various sections needed only to be set up according to the accompanying instruction chart.

PATHWAY TO PEACE

An exhibition prepared by the Disarmament Staff of the White House, handsomely mounted, and circulated free to cultural institutions around the country.

A display need not be elaborate to be successful. Simple designs are preferable, particularly for beginners.

A small library featuring Bible Week might show a facsimile of a Gutenberg Bible page (probably procurable from Philip C. Duschnes, 757 Madison Avenue, New York 21, N. Y.: Goodspeed's Book Shop, 18 Beacon Street, Boston 8, Mass., or Gutenberg Museum und Bibliothek, Rhein Allee, 3, Mainz, Germany). Along with this the exhibition might include Bibles of interest borrowed from persons in the community.

When planning an exhibit, decide upon the central idea, or theme of the display, then build around it. Make a rough preparatory sketch indicating layout and color treatment.

As most librarians are aware, Nicolas Jensen was a Frenchman who served an apprenticeship in the royal mint at Paris, and went to Mainz, Germany, where Gutenberg held forth, to learn the art of printing from movable type at the command of King Charles VII of France. Jensen expected to return to his native land, but following the King's death in 1461, he proceeded to Venice, and is thought by some authorities to have been that city's first printer.

Using Jensen as inspiration, an enterprising librarian could build a convincing display about the France and Italy of his period. No matter how seemingly distant the relationship, "the end justifies the means," and the worker with imagination will invariably find opportunities for linking displays with library services and resources.

AROUND THE WORLD IN 80 BOOKS

An exhibit prepared for a festival of the United Nations Association of Maryland, in cooperation with the Enoch Pratt Free Library's Office of Adult Services. Emphasizing literacy, the charts and signs centered on the theme, "If people can read . . . Books bring the world together."

Whatever the subject emphasized, in the selection of material it is usually wise to include a varied collection of literature, to interest as many types and ages as possible.

Color is a valuable element in any exhibit. When several tones are employed in the design they must harmonize or contrast, but never clash. Workers who claim they have no color sense can study magazine advertisements, as well as bus and trolley cards for pleasing combinations. In summer it is well to emphasize the cooler colors — blues, greens, grays, white, violet. During the winter months the warmer colors — reds, yellows, oranges, etc. — would naturally predominate.

Posters, picture maps, paper jackets on book discards, are always welcome additions to any exhibit, not only for their utilitarian value, but also for their liveliness of color. Photo-graphs, models, action devices, lend added interest.

When choosing literature for a display care must be taken to select books that can be shown to advantage. Good, readable spines, attractive covers and illustrations, clear print for easy reading are all factors to be considered. Often the outer binding of a book may be shabby and dull, but the frontispiece, end-papers or an inside illustration may be gay and inviting. It is up to the librarian to feature the best points of books used in an exhibit.

Whenever possible, book jackets should be used over dummy books — volumes worn out in active service, "freak" or outdated gift books not worth adding. Then the actual volumes may circulate on request. For if a borrower must wait for the publication desired until the display is dismantled, he may lose interest.

"DRESS-UP" DECORATIONS   *The appearance of many displays is improved by the use of gay cardboard strips, rectangles, triangles and squares arranged in appealing patterns to offset less colorful backdrop items. The cutter demonstrated here can take a full 28 x 44 inches sheet of cardboard. Circles up to 24 inches in diameter may be produced with a special attachment on the *Cutawl machine.*

(*See Preparation and Techniques).

PAINTING BULLETIN BOARDS AND DISPLAY BACKDROPS *For a smooth finish mix water paint well, and with a four-inch brush stroke the paint evenly up and down across the board. This will prevent streakiness.*

Every exhibit should have a backdrop that is eye-catching, to stop people in their tracks. The aim is to make each library exhibit so irresistible that passers-by, who read as they run, will come back for a second and longer look. At the Enoch Pratt Free Library portable insulite (wallboard) panels, reinforced with 2 by 4 wooden frames to prevent warping, are used for the purpose. Self-supporting on small wood feet, they are covered with quick-drying water paints and adorned with attractive books and related cardboard decorations.

Three-dimensional cutout letters, painted to set off the rest of the design, are carefully spaced out and measured for the caption or message.

As to arrangement, avoid clutter. It is well to remember that no matter how great the variety of pieces involved, the display must not appear crowded or jumbled. Each item should be placed so that it may be plainly seen. No one piece should be permitted to obscure another. The more significant books should be placed most strategically, but the entire exhibit must present a certain symmetry and balance.

There should always be sufficient "white space," to use the printer's term. For if an exhibit appears crowded or disjointed, it will hardly attract attention, much less create interest or stimulate the desire to read which, after all, is the primary purpose of the display.

After a display has been completed it should be examined carefully for flaws. Perhaps a book is upside down, a label out of line, or an object off balance. Minor adjustments are almost always necessary.

INSULITE DISPLAY PANELS *Such items are easy to construct. Insulite, a wood-pulp wall board ½ inch thick, can be purchased in almost any lumber yard, in 4 x 8 foot sheets. It takes paint and pins readily, but must be protected from knocks and bumps, as it chips and scars easily. A 2 x 4 frame on the back of the panel prevents warping. After the panel has been painted and decorated, free-standing feet may be bolted on, for greater stability.*

SELECTING CAPTION LETTERS

The amount of display space and the material to be featured determine the size and style of the caption letters. A large space naturally calls for larger letters, and bulky display pieces used in an exhibit also would demand big letters. On the other hand, fragile china or handmade jewelry would call for a caption composed of "refined," graceful letters. Shelves or boxes divided into compartments do nicely for storing letter alphabets.

PAINTING LETTERS

At the Enoch Pratt Free Library quick-drying water paints in colors that harmonize or contrast with other display features are used extensively for exhibits captions. If its edges are coated first, each letter can then be held on the palm of the hand and the face painted. Lay on a smooth, hard surface to dry.

SPACING OF LETTERS

Three-dimensional letters used in display captions must be evenly aligned and spaced out as meticulously as a page of hand-set type. A long, thin strip of wood temporarily tacked onto the working area below the letters, will keep the bottoms of the letters on an even keel. Spaces between letters, as well as spaces between words, should be equalized. (Letters placed on contrasting cardboard strips generally show up to advantage). Until experience has developed a "straight eye," a measuring guide should be used.

CHAPTER THREE

PREPARATION AND TECHNIQUES

Keeping in mind the keen competition for the public's attention these days, every library display must be attractive and eye-catching if it is to fulfill its function. This chapter will deal with some of the mechanics for achieving that aim. Materials mentioned may be checked in the appendix, under Sources of Supplies.

For instance, if two corners of a book jacket or leaflet are affixed firmly to a bulletin board with thumb tacks, while the remaining two flap loosely in the breeze every time the door opens, the display loses much of its appeal.

And speaking of thumb tacks — avoid using different colored heads on a single display

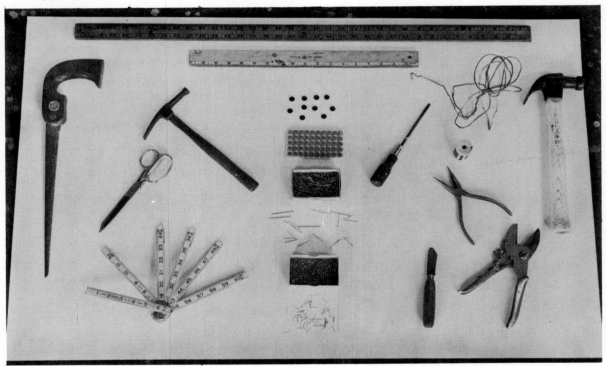

TOOLS OF THE TRADE   *Pictured here are a few simple working tools useful in the preparation of exhibits. Measurements should be accurate, neatness is indispensable.*

One of the first requirements of good display is neatness. Unless an exhibit is neat, it cannot look attractive, and if it is not attractive, it will not get attention. Certainly it goes without saying that unless an exhibit draws attention, it will hardly stimulate reading interest, with the result that most of the time and money spent in its preparation are virtually wasted.

piece! When a small white announcement is attached to a bulletin board with a red, a green, and two steel thumb tacks — as I have seen done — the result is nothing more than a hodgepodge. Don't use the more expensive but less attractive steel or brass tacks to make display pieces become joined to a surface, if you can obtain others which fit more harmoniously into the design. When thumb tacks are to show, get colors to match the display materials, or paint white ones the proper shade, so they will not be a disturbing factor.

If possible fasten things with pins (available in sizes ranging from ½ inch to 2 or more inches, depending on the requirements of the job at hand), and then touch up the tiny pinheads with matching paints, so that they will blend unobtrusively into the items featured.

BOOK DISPLAY EQUIPMENT

Examples of items used by the Enoch Pratt Free Library. Some are more than 25 years old.

AFTER DECORATION

Dummy books in paper jackets conceal most of the wooden pedestals and tables in Pratt Library displays.

Wooden boxes, pedestals, blocks — painted or varnished to suit the surroundings — and small wrought iron or wooden troughs, will serve admirably as book display fixtures. Vari-sized cartons and other containers, obtained from neighborhood stores likely to discard them, can be covered with odds and ends of wallpaper, gay wrapping paper, metal foil or low-priced cloth to make presentable book stands.

Ordinary metal book supports, placed at a 45 degree angle or bent to any other height desired, can also be pressed into service as "fixtures." But when adjoining books are placed on such supports, they should be at similar levels, for if one is projected higher than the other, the area will offer a ragged appearance.

In addition, book supports may be used straight to prop up books that have a tendency to fall over. Insert these in the back of the volumes, with the tongue-like base pointing toward the rear of the display, in line with the idea that "props" — devices by which material is shown to its best advantage — must always be as inconspicuous as possible.

Valuable manuscripts, old letters and other exhibits susceptible to the sun's rays, may be wrapped in amber cellophane to prevent fading. For a firm base and minimum buckling, place a piece of cardboard cut to size under each piece before wrapping.

Narrow white cotton tape, inexpensive when obtained in 1000-yard spools, is useful for tying books open. Cut two strips a little longer than twice the height of the book to be opened and place them on the outer margins, tying the ends at the back. Snip off the long ends, so they will not protrude. Make sure the tape strips are about ¼ inch from the edge, top

ATTACHING BOOKS WITH TAPE *Attaching a book to a bulletin board or display backdrop is a simple procedure. Insert narrow cotton tape between the paper jacket and front cover, knotting ends at center back. Then below and above the knot, as indicated, insert two upholstery tacks, pushing through the tape with points facing out. Snip off tape ends with scissors and press the book into the desired position, the points penetrating the backdrop. Two long pins placed beneath the book will keep it from sagging to right or left.*

and bottom. (Rubber bands, sometimes employed by librarians for this purpose, detract from the appearance of the book and have a tendency to break when temperatures mount, looking like so many worms on the floor of the exhibit.)

The narrow white tape is also useful for attaching books to display backdrops. In each case cut a length of tape somewhat longer than twice the height of the book. Slip it between the jacket and the front cover of the dummy book, pull taut and knot the tape ends at the center back of the book. Snip off excess ends. Above and below the knot, about six inches apart, insert two upholstery tacks, the points pushed through the tape and facing away from the book. Then press the volume onto the backdrop, in the position desired. Two steel pins

placed directly below the bottom book corners will prevent sagging and will help support the piece.

When working with specially fine books, or books with full-page illustrations, use ½ inch clear, non-adhesive plastic or acetate strips to hold the volumes open. These can be cut from material available in sheets of 40 x 60 inches, or by the yard. Place at page edges, instead of the white tape, and fasten ends at the back of each book with small metal OK clips available in stationery stores.

Occasionally a sheet of tissue paper protects the frontispiece of a book to be displayed, obscuring the illustration. After the book has been tied open, roll the tissue gently but tightly, and fasten it carefully to the center of the book with regular paper clips. The thinner

REINFORCING WITH CARDBOARD *To prevent curling, reinforce pamphlets, magazines, pictures, leaflets and newspaper clippings with cardboard. Two pieces, only very slightly smaller than page size, are inserted in each pamphlet or magazine. Clear, non-adhesive acetate strips cut into ½ inch widths are placed on the outer page edges, so as not to cover printing, and fastened with metal OK clips, holding the concealed cardboard in place. Except for single page items, when there is no alternative, OK clips should be placed where they will not show.*

part of the clip is inserted into the cigarette-type roll, top and bottom. Do not close the book after this treatment, as the tissue will crease. When the display is dismantled, remove the paper clips and flatten the tissue before removing the tapes and closing the book.

Flimsy pamphlets, pictures and newspaper clippings should be reinforced with cardboard before being placed in an exhibition, to prevent curling. To reinforce a pamphlet cut two pieces of old cardboard slightly smaller than page size. Place the colored side of the cardboard away from public view, thus insuring that it will not be conspicuous if the cardboard should slip a bit later. Cut two ½ inch wide clear plastic strips the desired length, and fasten with QK clips on the inside of the pamphlet if the cover is to be shown. When a pamphlet is to be opened, the OK clips should be at the back, in line with the need to conceal "props."

To reinforce an inexpensive photograph or flat paper, cut cardboard the exact size of the item. Fasten the four corners with small OK clips, the sharp prongs piercing the cardboard. Valuable materials may be tied with strips of the clear plastic tape at the outer edges (similar to those used on open books) with OK clips fastening the strips at the back.

If it is necessary for a piece thus handled to stand upright, attach to the reinforcement, center back, a strip of cardboard about 3 inches wide, flush with the bottom and about 2½ inches down from the top edge. Paste only the upper fourth of the strip, leaving the lower section as an easel.

To affix a photograph or picture to a bulletin

PROTECTING PICTURES *Valuable photographs, drawings and other pictorial items may be affixed to bulletin boards without puncturing holes in the corners. In each case, turn the display piece face down on a work table. Depending upon its weight, place thumb tacks or upholstery tacks at intervals near the edge all around, prongs pointing up, then cover the heads with strips of masking tape, as shown in the accompanying photograph. When the masking tape "border" is complete, the protruding points are pressed into position on the bulletin board.*

board without visible means and without puncturing holes in the corners, turn the display piece face down on a work table. Lay as many thumb tacks or upholstery tacks as seem necessary about 3 inches apart and about ½ inch from the edge all around, prongs pointing up. Then make a border with masking tape, covering the heads of the tacks and allowing only the sharp prongs to protrude. The picture can then be pressed into position on the bulletin board.

Persons without formal art training or talent can nevertheless turn out attractive display decorations by incorporating into the design enlargements of illustrations encountered in book jackets, books, magazines, pamphlets, posters or leaflets. Credit, of course, should always be given.

To enlarge a drawing by the squaring method, choose the illustration which you wish to present as the eye-catching device for your exhibit. Draw a perfect square around the illustration. Then with pencil and ruler divide this square into ½ inch squares.

Determine the size of the enlargement desired. If your backdrop illustration is to be four times the original size, then another square is drawn, four times the size of the first one. This time, with your pencil and ruler draw your lines at 2 inch intervals until the whole area is taken care of. Next, in the proportion of the original illustration, draw in your picture, block by block, as seen in the ½ inch squares. Do not worry about the overall pattern, but duplicate the lines in each square exactly, and the larger drawing will come out the same as the original. Cutouts, as well as drawings, can be done in this way.

On occasion, also, enlarged photostatic reproductions of sharp half-tones and black-and-white drawings make good display decorations when mounted on wallboard.

ENLARGING BY THE SQUARING METHOD

Small drawings found in books, magazines and pamphlets can be "blown up" effectively for posters and display decorations. By dividing the original into small squares and duplicating the individual block lines in proportionately bigger squares, an exact enlargement is achieved. Credit should always be given.

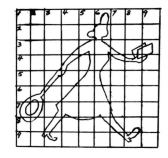

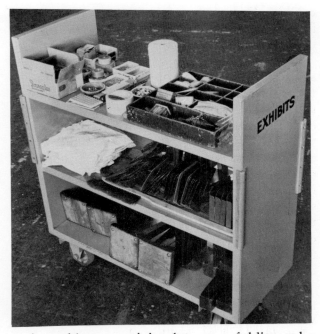

A workbox containing hammer, folding rule, pliers, scissors, dust cloths, thumb and upholstery tacks, assorted pins and nails, OK and paper clips, clear and cotton tape strips, touch-up paints, glue, art gum and other display paraphernalia is required equipment. Those libraries which can afford a Cutawl machine for cutting caption letters and display decorations, will find it a tremendous advantage over scissors, razor blades, knives and other elementary cutting tools. Taking material up to an inch in thickness, the Cutawl will produce at one time several sets of letters in 14-ply (⅛ inch) cardboard, as well as attractive designs related to books and reading, thereby greatly enhancing the exhibits.

Some cautions and reminders:

Exhibits should be designed and presented in such a way that they are self-explanatory

When fitting paper jackets on "dummy" books, be sure you have a snug fit — check for height, depth and width of spine, so that the volumes will appear genuine

To gain a three-dimensional effect with cardboard decorations, place pieces of insulite behind them and attach to the bulletin board or exhibits backdrop with long pins

WORK TRUCK

Equipment required for display preparation and installation is handy to use if assembled compactly in an accessible spot. A book truck, if available, serves admirably for this purpose, as it can be moved at will.

Bend pin points over with pliers where they protrude dangerously. Do not let insulite edges show

Remove and file book cards of actual books used in displays, with a note as to when the displays are to be dismantled, in order to answer inquiries and take reserves from readers

Keep a record of all exhibits by lender, subject, date

Have a "possibilities" file of material offered for loan, for future reference

Save all signs, posters, letters, decorations, cardboard circles, triangles, etc., for later showings in somewhat different form

Take good care of equipment, storing it properly when not in use

CUTAWL MACHINE

Display decorations in almost every conceivable pattern can be made with the versatile Cutawl machine. Patterns may be drawn on brown wrapping paper, and laid over the material to be cut. A few pins driven in will hold both in place during the cutting process. The chisel-like "knife" is guided along the drawn lines. The Cutawl will take material up to an inch in thickness, and special blades for cutting wood and metal are available. If the design is to include several colors, the pieces can be put together like a jigsaw puzzle, with gummed paper on the back. To prevent warping, cover the finished cutout with clean paper, weight down, and press overnight.

CHAPTER FOUR

POSTERS, SIGNS AND SHOWCARDS

Just as a chain is no stronger than its weakest link, so an exhibit is no better than its posters, signs and showcards. Regardless of how many fine features a display may boast, inferior posters and lettering will lower the level of the effort, spoiling the overall effect and leaving viewers with a bad impression.

placed in such a way that comprehension is quick and clear. Color masses must be pleasing, well-balanced.

Libraries lacking competent art staff or volunteer artists, may want to invest in an enlarging projector — such as that put out by the Beseler Company — for "blowing up" suitable

IN PRAISE OF POSTERS

Posters are the hardy perennials of library displays. If well executed they serve to win attention and to stimulate interest in books and reading. Color, size, design and lettering are the principal elements to consider. In addition to paints, charcoal, crayons and the other familiar media, novel effects may be achieved by using construction paper scissor-cutouts for illustrations (attached with rubber cement) and adding ink-line finishing touches. The poster in foreground is an example of the latter treatment.

Posters, signs and showcards used in an exhibit should supplement and tie in with the principal caption. Together they tell the library's story, and carry the message.

After determining the size and color preference of each piece as part of the whole, consider the design, or layout. Design is an orderly plan of arrangement. It guides the eye from one element to another, with stopping places for emphasis, to a logical climax. The words and illustrations should be grouped and

illustrations available in their collections. (Some of these gadgets also reduce the size of pictures when such treatment is desired.)

Novices in poster art may also find helpful the instructions on enlarging drawings by the squaring method, given in the chapter, PREPARATION AND TECHNIQUES.

All hand-lettering must be distinct, direct and easy to read, with minimum wordage necessary to accomplish its purpose. The style should conform as far as possible to the exhibits

INFORMATION ATTRACTIVELY PRESENTED

Descriptive showcards, signs and labels call for special skills and talents. The competent showcard writer is usually a versatile artist who varies his pen and brush lettering styles to suit the exhibits being offered. Under no circumstances should crude, "home-made" signs and explanatory notes be used in a library display. They will counteract the good impression created by the exhibit proper.

When professionally-done, hand-lettered labels are not obtainable, typed ones may be used. Space with care, and see that the typewriter ribbon is in good condition, for maximum legibility.

theme. For example, a Shakespearean display would call for a variation of Old English lettering, while a show devoted to abstract art would demand modern lettering. Copy should be "short and snappy" — brief enough to be read quickly, and interesting enough to win and hold attention.

Librarians whose budgets can stand the strain would be wise to have experts do their lettering work, if they have no way of getting free professional assistance. Often showcard writers in department stores or free lance display workers will take on such added chores, to make extra money in their spare time. In this way the library gets the benefit of reduced rates. Once you have conveyed your ideas to an experienced sign and poster man, given him the copy and indicated sizes, let him use his own initiative. The chances are he will improve considerably on your suggestions.

For those who wish to investigate other possibilities there are available lettering guides, such as the Wrico lettering stencils, and the expensive card-writing equipment — Showcard Machine, Lino-O-Scribe and Print-A-Sign.

On occasion three-dimensional cutout letters may be employed successfully for poster messages. These letters can be acquired for pennies.

Alphabets are obtainable in various sizes, styles and materials. For libraries forced to practice rigid economy it is generally good policy to limit purchase to one style. Variety may be achieved by combining two or three sizes of the same type.

Cheapest and perhaps most useful for the library display purposes are the durable die-cut letters. These range from the very thin Mutual Aids, adhesive and non-adhesive, to the thicker Hallcraft, Redicut and others. They may be had in special fonts or sets, with the proper assortment of vowels and consonants, for adequate service. Some choice of color is available, and in a few cases purchasers may order script letters as well as Roman; lowercase letters, as well as capitals.

GIFT POSTERS *For special campaigns outside agencies and individuals can sometimes be persuaded to underwrite poster projects. Hundreds of copies of this poster were donated by The Joseph Katz Company, Advertising, for the Enoch Pratt Free Library's first branch bond issue in Baltimore.*

(Photo courtesy of The Baltimore Sunpapers)

CHAPTER FIVE

TIPS TO TEACHERS

School teachers and teacher-librarians have a wonderful opportunity, as well as a great responsibility. It lies within their province not only to teach children how to read, but also how to think.

Young minds are curious, receptive minds. It is up to teachers and librarians to feed them a nutritious mental diet. Boys and girls who learn to read with discrimination early in life, generally grow into good citizens, mature in thought and action.

Visual displays are now ranked among the foremost educational aids. Classroom, as well as library exhibits, can be arranged in such a way as to tell an interesting story. History and geography can be made dramatic and colorful for the student who despises both. Zoology can be made appealing to the girl who squirms at the mere mention of a worm. Through effective exhibits even the "driest" subjects can become understandable and arresting.

Who knows but that it may be a book in

POSTER TRANSFORMED

The family group in this "home" setting originally appeared on a poster issued by a manufacturer of light bulbs. Strips of donated wallpaper were used for the background, and the "curtains" were made from shelf paper bought in the five-and-dime store.

one of your displays that will light the spark of scientific discovery in a boy, and inspire him to become a benefactor of mankind? Pasteur, Westinghouse and many other notables were spurred to their achievements by reading.

A sure-fire method of producing a popular school exhibit is to show objects loaned by pupils or their parents. Encourage such cooperation, drawing on selective handicraft and hobby collections. Get your art classes interested, and if there are shop courses in your school some boys handy with tools will gladly assist with the project.

Participation intensifies interest. If it seems feasible, appoint an exhibition committee. The students can help plan and prepare the displays, and by pooling ideas and resources, you may get some valuable support. Change the personnel of your committee periodically, in order to give as many youngsters as possible an opportunity to share actively in the program. More and more they will come to feel a personal responsibility for the exhibits, and their interest and enthusiasm will grow proportionately.

Naturally the children will discuss the displays in their homes, and among their friends. The popularity of the exhibits will mount accordingly. In addition, if you can accommodate visitors, inform neighborhood individuals and groups that would not ordinarily hear about the show.

In the event of a special Shakespearean display, for example, notify local literary clubs. Post notices about your exhibit on the bulletin boards of churches in your area, on store counters, at fairs, and wherever else numbers of people are likely to see them.

By all means get reports of your exhibit into the daily and weekly newspapers. There is a good deal of truth in the old saying, "Nothing succeeds like success." Accounts of your exhibits in the newspapers will impress readers with the importance of what you are doing.

CASE DISPLAY

Locomotive models augment the showing of railroad books for children.

Children's librarians report that boys and girls prefer exhibits projecting things and topics that are familar. They also welcome dramatic, imaginative arrangements, and appreciate well-planned, attractively-presented though simple, exhibits.

Central characters denoting action are always juvenile favorites. Color is important. At the Enoch Pratt Free Library two extremes in intensity seem to register well — pale pastels combined with deep, vibrant tones. Youngsters appear to favor neat, crisp, uncluttered displays and posters, with captions short and to the point.

A successful display recently reported by the Edmondson Avenue Branch featured "MEN OF IRON." This dramatized two 10″ figurines, knights in battle. One, vanquished, was lying prone, his shield and sword beside him. The victor, bending over the fallen man, stood with sword raised, ready to give the final thrust. Books on chivalry were placed at strategic points. The knights wore armor fashioned from aluminum foil, and the banner and backdrop were deep purple. Cutout silver letters comprised the caption.

"CIRCUS DAYS" was the title of an exhibit depicting miniature clowns equipped with the oversize wooden shoes characteristic of real clowns. The head of one Big Top jester was seen bursting through a drum.

A spooky "GHOSTS AND GOBLINS" display contained store-bought Hallowe'en masks — a devil and a ghost with streamer confetti — along with appropriate books. According to Mrs. Freda Freyer, children's librarian, "It was the shivery-looking caption-letters cut from cardboard by the Exhibits staff, that did the trick. We use them from year to year."

Youngsters enjoy sly humor behind ideas and captions. For her display, "IT'S NEARLY SPRING," Mrs. Freyer used letters spelling out the theme above a book bin decorated with a picture from an old *Jack and Jill* Magazine. The illustration showed an elf protecting himself from the rain by holding a toadstool umbrella. When, later, the vernal equinox occurred, Mrs. Freyer superimposed a large paper X on the heading's middle word, thus deleting the "nearly." Commented some of the youthful patrons, "Say, that's plenty neat."

GINGERBREAD HOUSE

At the Enoch Pratt Free Library's Edmondson Avenue Branch this "Hansel and Gretel" cake-and-candy structure added considerable interest to a display of fairy and folk tales.

(Photo by Walter McCardell, The Sunpapers, Baltimore).

46

From time to time children enjoy "quiet" arrangements — displays devoid of apparent action stimulus, but pleasant to look at. A cake-and-candy "gingerbread" house reminiscent of Hansel and Gretel, as a foil for fairy and folk tales, is worth all the time and effort expended. Beatrix Potter figurines — Peter Rabbit and the rest — are always well received.

Those teachers who cannot create authentic-looking three-dimensional replicas of book characters, gingerbread houses and similar items for exhibits, or who cannot obtain them from other sources, may resort to using paper silhouettes, which are easy to make.

In connection with a display of books about Columbus and other explorers, Mrs. Freyer cut white paper silhouettes of the Nina, the Pinta and Santa Maria. She placed these in progression of size — to create the illusion of sailing into the distance — on deep blue paper with pristine white letters spelling out the caption, "SAIL ON."

Seasonal displays usually have a host of admirers. At the Edmondson library "I LIKE WINTER" combined a vivid blue background with lots of white: snow, snowballs, snow men, snow crystals cut from dull white paper. Icicles dripped from the caption letters.

Frequently pictorial art in giveaway posters can be cut and mounted attractively for bulletin boards and display backdrops. United Nations posters are among those which adapt particularly well to this treatment.

Catchy book titles often make good display captions. For example, the exhibit "MEN OF IRON" was taken from Howard Pyle's book of the same title, and "I LIKE WINTER" was suggested by Lois Lenski's well-known volume.

Exhibiting collection or hobby items always brings offers of additional material. Children enjoy collections of dolls, stamps, sea shells, puppets, almost anything. Another child's work is always meaningful to youngsters. Related

WALLPAPER COSTUME

Simple display designs appeal to children. The girl's wallpaper dress was easy to cut and pin, and paper doilies provided the "lace" trimming."

POSTER CUTOUTS

Many attractive display designs can be contrived with a little resourcefulness. This backdrop center piece was cut from a United Nations poster duplicating the one illustrated.

articles supplementing the books invariably serve as "bait" to draw attention.

For an exhibit in Baltimore involving David Livingstone, the Scottish explorer, an African shield, spears, war hatchet, bow, arrows and quiver were borrowed. A display centering on "ALICE IN WONDERLAND" included puppets representing various characters in the story. Stuffed and mounted birds, nests and eggs were obtained for an exhibit devoted to bird habits and habitats.

Do not hesitate to request the loan of such material. Local individuals and groups are unfailingly cooperative, particularly where the education of children is concerned. Of course, all borrowed properties must be handled with scrupulous care, and returned safely to the owners.

Following are some additional display topics which have appealed to Baltimore boys and girls: astronomy; the story of transportation; sports; photography; wild flowers; historic trails across the United States; camping; paper making; fossils; rockets; bees; foreign trade; Indian artifacts; bird houses; current events; the story of spices; poisonous plants; patents; sea stories; steel; bottle making; marionettes; minerals; prehistoric animals; care of pets; the National Parks; safety; Eskimos; weather.

Mrs. Freyer sums it all up this way: "The philosophy of trying to achieve effective exhibits with the two-fold purpose of providing entertainment and promoting good books is to have colorful, simple displays, with an occasional elaborate one sandwiched in when a busy schedule permits.

"Think about what you want to 'sell'; decide when is the right time to present the display. Be aware, ahead of time, of neighborhood interests and activities, holidays, seasons, events that you may care to observe, always tying in with appropriate reading. Then present the ideas in ways that you know are appealing to young minds."

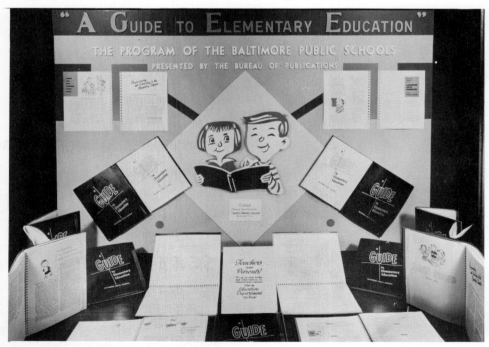

FOR TEACHERS AND PARENTS *The Enoch Pratt Free Library works closely with Baltimore's public schools, displaying their publications of widespread interest. For their part, the public schools list important library exhibits and activities in their calendar of events, and cooperate in many other ways.*

CHAPTER SIX

LIBRARY BOOK FAIRS

Library book fairs are handled in many ways, depending on the resources of the sponsoring agency, and the apparent needs of the community.

For those desiring to set up an elaborate installation, with two or three thousand new books for children and adults, it would be desirable to obtain the financial and promotional sponsorship of a local newspaper. Publishers and local bookstores are likely to lend books needed, and to arrange for the appearance of prominent authors whose names are sure to attract visitors. Others may help with the decorations, promotional literature and additional activities. A big book fair is a big undertaking, and requires many heads and hands.

To date the Enoch Pratt Free Library has held book fairs in schools and within the library. Under the able direction of Mrs. Margaret A. Edwards, coordinator of work with young adults, the most successful ones have been staged in the city's secondary schools.

Some years ago Miss Grace P. Slocum, now Mrs. Edwards' counterpart in the Brooklyn Public Library, but formerly one of her Pratt aides, recounted the fair's beginnings in the *Library Journal*. She said, in part:

"In the Patterson Park area of East Baltimore, where children read some, young people read little and adults read even less, the neighborhood branch librarian approached the head of the English department of the nearby high school to consider how the seniors could be

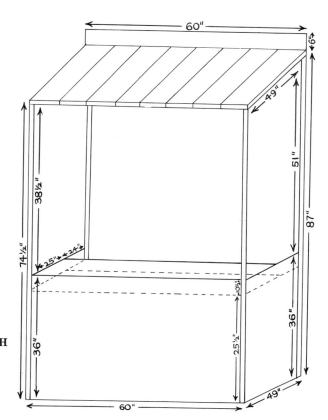

PORTABLE BOOK FAIR BOOTH

Of the type used by the Enoch Pratt Free Library.

made aware of what the public library could offer them after they left school. Something more was needed than book talks in the classrooms in this community, where many students had never set foot in the library. Tentative plans were therefore made for the English classes to visit the branch during school hours.

"Obviously, a routine program on library use would bore these seniors to death. A light touch was needed. A carnival type show seemed to be the answer.

in the rear. Of the 49 inches in depth, 25 were used for a counter under which was built a shelf for extra books, and the remaining 24 inches were left for standing room (for a 'Y' librarian). Each booth was painted a different color and covered with green and red striped awning top.

"The downstairs meeting room of the branch where the fair was to be held had recently been painted, but the exposed steam pipes and radiators suspended midway up the walls pre-

DECORATED BOOK FAIR BOOTH

The gay striped awning top and colorful decorations help create a carnival-like atmosphere, setting the stage for the book display.

"The library carpenter built eight collapsible booths which could easily be disassembled and stored for future use. The booths measured 60 inches across and 74½ inches high in front, the roof sloping up to a height of 87 inches

sented problems. By cutting strips of crepe paper two inches wide, in three different colors, an attractive plaid design covered the pipes, making an effective border around the top of the room.

"Balloons were hung from the ancient, unsightly light fixtures. Thus lighted up, the balloons seemed to be incandescent. Three booths were lined up on either side of the room, with the remaining two back to back in the center. The hobby table was placed in an alcove at the rear of the auditorium; the stage at the front was used for the music and dance exhibit. A storeroom nearby was used for the party display.

"On the Monday morning when the first class of seniors arrived at 9 o'clock, they were surprised to be asked to go downstairs, and still more surprised when they began to hear the opening music from 'An American in Paris.' Balloons, serpentine and crepe paper streamers,

along with booths and music, created a carnival atmosphere. Leaflets announcing the Carnival of Books and listing the library's services were handed out at the door. On the back of the handbills was a notice that a prize would be given away each day — any book in the fair costing $5.00 or less — to the person presenting the best reason for wanting the book.

"The Patterson Park assistant, as M.C., stood on the stage and pointed out each booth where the 'Y' librarian in charge briefly explained his part of the show. After reminding the seniors to try for the prize, and saying that any of the books . . . could be borrowed on either a student's name or his card, the M.C. declared the carnival officially opened.

"SALES PITCH" TO YOUNG ADULTS *The Pratt Library's book fair has become a "Baltimore institution" in the city's high schools, with hundreds of seniors attending annually.*

"The backdrop of the first booth, *Choosing a Career,* featured the cutout of a mother kangaroo whose young son had been riding free too long. At the end of her patience, she was demanding, 'Don't you think it's time you got yourself a job?' Here were displayed up-to-date pamphlets and books on vocations and opportunities in the armed forces.

"In the booth, *Personality Merry-Go-Round,* a revolving carousel carried gold horses and books on etiquette and psychology, the best in dating and family living.

"Red brick paper and English ivy decorated the college booth where catalogs from 75 colleges and universities could be borrowed, with information on how to select a school, or why go to college. Guides for the 'prom-trotter' and a collection of new college stories were included with the more serious material."

Design for Living introduced the booth on home decoration and planning efficiency; *Laugh Like Anything* was the humor caption; *Anyone Can Paint* presented fine arts publications; *Ride Your Hobby* offered literature ranging from stamp collecting to taxidermy.

All Sinners This Way led to a "sinner's party" in the storeroom, following directions from Van Rensselaer's "Party Book," with ghosts, goblins and devils appended to the walls of storage shelves, and a cutout of St. Peter guarding the keys to the Pearly Gate of Heaven.

"The heads of the English departments in all the city's high schools," Miss Slocum explained, "were invited to the carnival. They came, some expecting to find a well-meant but amateurish show, but remained charmed by the air of sophistication and the displays of an almost professional tone. But more than that, they were pleased — as the library staff was pleased — to find young people in a community generally thought to be made up of non-readers, handling books with interest and finding in them ideas related not only to their present daily interests, but also to their future lives."

As a result of that first experiment, the fair has become an annual fixture in Baltimore's high schools. The usual procedure is for the Office of Work with Young Adults to contact the high school librarians and principals through the supervisor of libraries for the Baltimore Department of Education. After blanket approval is obtained a schedule is made up allowing one to three days for each school, depending on enrollment, with all twelfth grade classes visiting the fair for one period each.

Ray M. Fry, at present librarian of the Rosenberg Library in Galveston, Texas, and formerly one of Mrs. Edwards' assistants, has thus described the event in an article for *Top of the News,* published by the Young Adult Services Division and the Children's Services Division of the American Library Association:

"Barnum and Bailey comes only in the spring, but the high school book fair of the Enoch Pratt moves from school to school within the city from October until June. In a setting of bright colors, informality and gay music . . . the show has become traditional.

"To the music of *Gaite Parisienne* the students converge for the fair which today, let us imagine, has been assembled in the library annex at coeducational Forest Park High School. Eight brilliantly decorated booths are spaced around the room and dozens of pennants crisscross the center. As the students enter, they immediately begin browsing, and each seems to be attracted by the caption on at least one of the booths. The ringmaster, one of the more experienced young adult librarians, and top banana for today's performance, signals for attention as the fair is officially opened.

" 'When you complete high school,' she begins, 'most of you are going to do one of three things: you will continue your schooling, you will get married, or you will go to work. Whether you are trying to balance the family budget, applying for a graduate fellowship in physics, or looking for aids to help you get ahead in your vocation, remember that the Enoch Pratt Free Library can help you.

" 'Don't think that when you finish high school your public library loses its usefulness for you. Suppose you are going to college. Let the "barker" on my right tell you about the college booth. And remember, there are booklists at each booth for you. Perhaps if you can't get the book you want now, or you want more than the two books allowed, or you don't have time to read the book now, the list will be a convenient reminder at a later date. And now to Mr. X.'

"The crowd shifts its attention and the No. 1 Barker begins: 'In this pennant-infested booth there are all types of books about colleges and college life. Here is a book, "Should You Go to College?", that just might help you decide whether or not to attend. And Lovejoy's "College Guide" contains pertinent facts about 2,049 institutions of higher learning. Or, if you want a fictional approach to college life that tells of sororities and fraternities, why not read, "Take Care of My Little Girl" or "The Charmed Circle"?'

" 'Barker No. 1 continues his promotions for a few moments and then directs the crowd to the next booth.

" 'In this *Design for Living* booth,' Barker No. 2 announces, 'there are books for future homemakers . . . books on decorating, cooking, living within your income, and making simple electrical and plumbing repairs.' Mr. 'Y' is careful to display the books as he talks about them and points out specific recipes, party plans, and directions for making slip covers. The ringmaster then takes charge again to 'bark' the *Career* booth.

" 'Most of you will have to go to work within the next few years unless you can break yourself of the bad habit of eating,' she begins, 'and we have many books which will aid you in selecting the most suitable vocation or profession. Here is one called, "The Young Woman in Business." On page 12 the author has an interesting list of employee services which you should know about in estimating the salary for a prospective job. And this book, "How to Get and Hold the Job You Want," has a good chapter on how to analyze yourself as to business experience, ability and personality.'

"The 'barking' continues from booth to booth until the circuit is complete. Today, be-

VISITORS'-EYE-VIEW *This pre-Christmas book fair at the Pratt Library's main building suggested books as gifts for readers of all ages and walks of life. Members of the staff were on hand to discuss the books exhibited.*

sides those already mentioned, there is a *For Men Only* booth with war novels, handbooks for technicians, books for the home handyman, and adventure books. *Bell Ringers,* with outstanding novels of yesterday and today, is always a popular booth attractively decorated as it is with large bells. The remaining displays include a cart of international books called, *The World on the Move.*

"After all the booths have been introduced, the students are given about 30 minutes to select a book or two to take along, and we are ready for the next class.

"Whether a student takes a book, a booklist, or just the idea that Enoch Pratt has a book to suit his every need and interest, we believe that the book fair with its carnival atmosphere is making an impression on the high school students in Baltimore . . . With each fair we gain new friends, help old friends discover new interests, and convince the outgoing seniors that the library has informational and recreational reading that can play a vital part in their work and play as long as they live."

Of course, book fairs involve much hard work and are time-consuming. But when planned and staged with imagination and ingenuity, as a device for stimulating reader-interest, they have few equals.

BALTIMORE BOOKSELLERS   *Cooperated by displaying Book Fair posters and distributing the library's Christmas book lists.*

CHAPTER SEVEN

LIGHTING

Relatively few libraries are equipped with modern lighting for proper presentation of exhibits. Since many library displays have their largest attendance at night, it is often necessary to supplement existing electrical facilities with temporary installations, for more satisfactory viewing by visitors. Sometimes the addition of a few simple spotlights, well-placed, will make a world of difference.

Most power companies provide free advisory service to individuals and agencies seeking help with such problems. But for the benefit of workers who may not have access to the utilities, the following information, provided by G. Wilson Younglove, senior illuminating engineer for the Baltimore Gas and Electric Company, is offered.

Well-planned lighting for a display increases

PROJECTOR AND REFLECTOR LAMPS

Seen here are some of the many inexpensive light sources adaptable for use in either fixed or temporary display arrangements.

(Courtesy Large Lamp Department, General Electric Company, Cleveland, Ohio)

its power to attract attention and makes it easier to examine the items shown. This fact is well-known to supermarket managers, who have found that the same merchandise will sell several times faster to impulse buyers when displayed on a special spotlighted fixture, than it does in its accustomed place on the shelves.

The amount of light which an object reflects determines its visibility. In general, the brightness or quantity of light reflected should be from two to five times that of the surroundings in order to attract attention.

It is a good rule to avoid placing very dark and very light objects near each other if they are equally important to a lighted display. For example, a book jacket in glossy black with bold, wide-stroke blue letters could be very effective, but shown beside pastel-colored jackets would lose effectiveness unless it was spotlighted with many times as much light as its highly reflective associates.

On the market are a variety of inexpensive light sources readily adaptable for use in either fixed or temporary displays. Reflectorized incandescent lamps are available in sizes from 30 watts for small displays, to 500 watt or larger sealed beam lamps with assorted patterns.

The illustration on the preceding page shows some of these. In addition, there is the relatively new 30 watt R 20. Similar in appearance to the 75 watt R 30, but only $3\frac{15}{16}$ inches long and $2\frac{9}{16}$ inches in bulb diameter, this fixture is small enough to be concealed behind the hand. Where concealment of "props" is vital, the advantage is obvious.

The most popular of these lamps have standard screw thread bases and can be used in most adjustable sockets and hoods, a feature which permits their attachment almost anywhere. Others are like automobile headlamps, and require special housing.

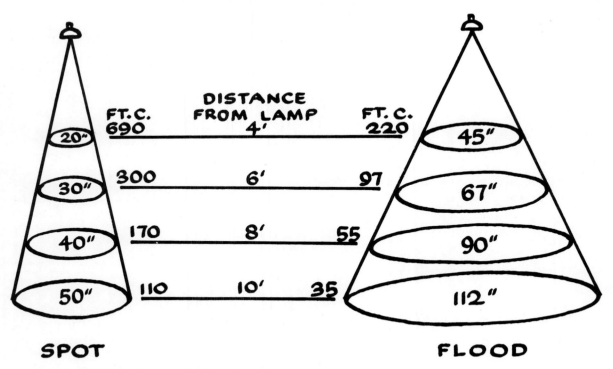

SPOT **FLOOD**

PROGRESSIVE LIGHT INTENSITY *Showing maximum amount of light and size of spot for several distances from 150 Watt PAR 38 Lamps. Light intensity at edge will be about ¼ that in center.*

The foregoing chart illustrates the area and light intensity which can be expected at progressive distances from some of the lamps. Since all incandescent illumination produces a considerable amount of infrared energy which upon absorption produces heat, care must be used, particularly with higher wattage lamps placed at close range to fragile books and other valuable items. Heat is extremely harmful to vellum, leather, ivories, painted and illuminated pages.

Because fluorescent lamps produce two to three times as many units of light per watt as do incandescent lamps, they often are preferred in show cases or other confined spaces where heat presents a problem. However, the light from fluorescent tubes cannot be controlled as can that from filament lamps, and they are therefore more frequently used for general area lighting, rather than for accenting. There is, however, a reflectorized fluorescent lamp available in either 40 inch or 96 inch length, which is satisfactory for lighting show cases, wall cases, shelf displays, and similar areas, since about 60 per cent more light is emitted from one side of the tube than from the other (see over).

When colors of the materials on display are important, it becomes necessary to use discretion in the selection of light sources. Incandescent light, which practically all people are accustomed to and accept, produces all colors in a continuous spectrum, but has a preponderance of yellow. With fluorescent lamps, however, the color of the light emitted is dependent on the combination of powdered chemical phosphors used to coat the inside of the tube. Since all presently known phosphors which emit red radiation are relatively low in efficiency, and since the early research in fluorescent lamps rather naturally sought maximum efficiencies, most of the tubes were lacking in red radiation.

For this reason color rendition was poor in the early fluorescent tubes, with all of the yellow-orange-red tones distorted and grayed. A "soft white" tube was then developed, particularly for use in the display of red meats, butter, produce and other foods, which had

been hitherto unacceptable to buyers because of the greenish-gray appearance that they took on under the early fluorescent tubes. However, "soft white" has a pinkish cast, and is therefore limited in its application.

Accordingly, two deluxe tubes have been introduced which, although somewhat lower in efficiency, produce either a warm white or a cool white light, as the result of the addition of enough red to give good color rendition. Together with standard warm white and cool white, they cover practically all display requirements.

In wall cases or for lighting objects displayed on shelves where it is necessary to keep the cross-section of light to a minimum in order to avoid obscuring displays, there are fluorescent show case channels just large enough to support the sockets and carry the necessary wires — approximately 1 x 2 inches, including the fluorescent tube. Under such circumstances the bulky ballast, an essential part of the circuit of all lamps depending on an electric arc, is remotely located in the base of the case or in an adjoining room. This is especially advantageous in libraries where ballast noise could be annoying.

When arranging lighting for a display, either incandescent or fluorescent, it is essential that the source of light be located for best treatment of surfaces to be observed both from a distance and at close range. Here the exhibits worker with a knowledge of stage lighting techniques has a valuable aid, for just as spotlights from the auditorium, and border lights, and spots overhead and behind the proscenium arch provide excellent vertical and horizontal illumination for a theatrical production, so, too, do they for displays.

If the exhibit includes highly polished material, it is only necessary to remember the law of optics which states that the angle of the reflected ray will be equal to the angle of the ray of light striking the surface from a normal to the reflecting surface (next drawing).

Lighting show windows represents a particularly difficult problem because of the reflection in the plate glass of buildings across the way,

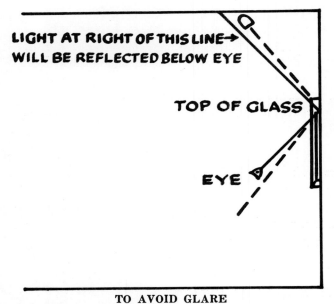

TO AVOID GLARE

Lighting a glass-covered picture so as to avoid reflected glare.

as well as of the cars and people on the street. It is extremely difficult to compete with illumination values of from 5,000 to 10,000 foot candles outside the window. The lighter the display background, the less disturbing the reflections will be. With open back windows and interior illumination of 50 to 100 foot candles, which is extremely good, the problem

is still difficult. With interior illumination of 5 foot candles or less, quite common in older buildings, show window reflections cannot be overcome except by the extensive use of large areas of highly reflective vertical background materials to compete with the high outside light levels.

Fluorescent lighting can be used to provide these high background brightnesses, but incandescent spotlighting is more effective for lighting the display itself, because spot beams can provide highlights, accents and interest which the flat lighting of fluorescent tubing cannot do. On occasion the real attraction value of a display may depend on highlights and shadows, light patterns, centers of focus, textures and color.

Interior displays offer infinite variety and challenge to the ingenuity of the exhibitor. A reflectorized lamp in a gaily-painted fruit juice can, with due regard for safety and fire protection requirements, can make the difference between a book on a shelf and an interest-compelling display. The chart below indicates what can be done with a 4 foot asymmetric fluorescent light strip, with the light bracketed at various distances from the vertical display panel. This is particularly applicable to dis-

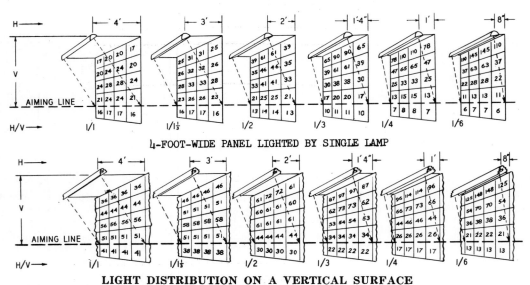

LIGHT DISTRIBUTION ON A VERTICAL SURFACE

Indicating probable effects of a 4 foot fluorescent light strip on a bulletin board type display. (Courtesy Large Lamp Department, General Electric Company, Cleveland, Ohio)

plays of such materials as maps, pamphlets and photographs. The chart shows the degree of uniformity of light distribution which can reasonably be expected.

Glass display cases present another problem which can be handled by mounting the light source in or on the upper front edge. A conventional show case fixture for fluorescent tubes is best suited. However, the reflectorized fluorescent lamp mentioned earlier can be used, and an extremely low-cost incandescent lamp known as T 10 RFL, available in 25 watt and 40 watt sizes, frequently does a good job. This is a filament lamp about 6 inches long, inserted and silver-coated on half the tubular envelope. in a T or tubular bulb, 1¼ inches in diameter. Mounted in a porcelain medium base socket, it provides the display worker with a wide variety of interesting applications. Aluminum foil also makes a good reflector. With a little ingenuity and a few cents, the display worker can sometimes create lighting miracles.

In the matter of rare or fragile books and objects, great care must be exercised to provide a safe environment. There is probably no greater authority on this subject than the United States Bureau of Standards, whose personnel have studied all factors affecting the preservation of such priceless documents as the Constitution and the Declaration of Independence. They report greater damage caused by blue light in the spectrum than by the red. The relative probable rate of damage from lighting of equal intensity is given:

Zenith sky light	100
Overcast sky	31.7
Sunlight	16.5
Fluorescent	
Cool white deluxe	11.5
Warm white deluxe	9.2
Incandescent	2.8

Glass and plastic filters are available to reduce the rate of damage, most of which involves fading or discoloration, brittleness or disintegration. Information on their effectiveness can be obtained from the Bureau of Standards, Washington 25, D.C.

By using imagination and inventiveness, library workers can meet almost any lighting challenge, with the result that many a dull-looking, difficult-to-view exhibit will be transformed into an effective instrument for the dissemination of knowledge.

INTERIOR CASE LIGHTING

Good lighting adds immeasurably to the value of exhibits. But problems of glare and light diffusion inside glass cases are often difficult to overcome. The Free Library of Philadelphia has found this type satisfactory.

EXTERIOR CASE LIGHTING

In areas where library lighting is poor, standard fluorescent light fixtures make displays more meaningful to visitors.

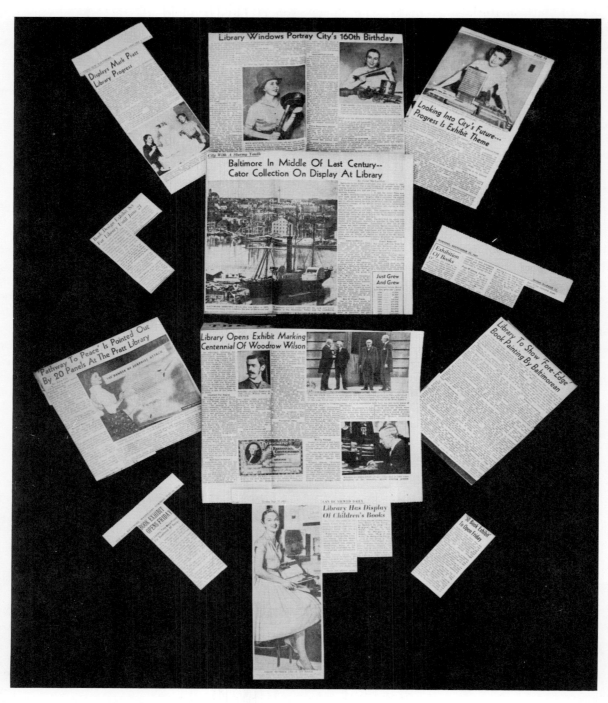

PRESS PROMOTION *Library displays may be covered at length in news stories, illustrated features and special columns. In addition, they should be listed briefly, whenever possible, in calendars of events and art gallery exhibits notices.*

CHAPTER EIGHT

PROMOTION IS A "MUST"

Preparing an exhibit is only part of the job. One must also promote it. For what advantage is there in setting up an effective, informative display if it is seen only by a relatively few people and only those few are stimulated by it to do additional reading?

Therefore, the librarian must reach out into the community through all available means — newspapers, television, radio, church bulletins, farm and labor publications, house organs, school papers and others affording free coverage — to announce the event and report some of its more interesting features.

The press publicity should start as soon as plans for the show are well in hand. Brief at first, the releases should lengthen as the opening date approaches, until the buildup reaches its climax with the actual "unveiling."

Notwithstanding the gains of other mass media in recent years, newspaper publicity remains the best type of promotion for libraries, since newspapers reach more people than any other single medium.

Stories should always be written from the reader's, rather than from the library's, point of view. Follow as closely as possible the style of the newspapers to which the items are submitted.

ATTRACTIVE "BAIT" *A pretty girl always adds interest to newspaper photographs calling attention to library displays.* (Courtesy The Baltimore Sunday American)

Here are a few elementary rules of journalism:

1. Type story on plain white paper, 8½ x 11 inches, double or triple-spaced, one side only. The typescript must be sharp and clear.
2. In upper left-hand corner put the sender's name, address and telephone number, so that the editor or his aide can verify or expand copy forwarded with minimum effort.
3. If at any time a special release date is desired, put FOR RELEASE ON ...., 19....... (exact date) in upper right-hand corner of Page 1.
4. Start copy one-third down on the page, leaving wide margins and indentations.
5. Use simple words, short sentences and paragraphs.
6. Do not hyphenate words at end of line, but place on next line when space is insufficient for completion.
7. Check facts, names, initials and titles carefully, to insure accuracy.
8. Give all pertinent information (answering the reporter's Five W's — Who, What, Why, When and Where) in the first paragraph, elaborating in subsequent paragraphs.
9. When release runs to more than one page, write (more) at lower right of each sheet of continuation.
10. Indicate article's end by placing number symbol # (single or multiple) several spaces below the final paragraph, center.

Copy to the various other publications should go out well in time for the editors' deadlines, ascertained in advance.

In connection with exhibits more elaborate and ambitious than usual, related posters may be distributed for placement in the windows or interiors of drugstores, groceries, restaurants, laundries, fire houses and similar establishments.

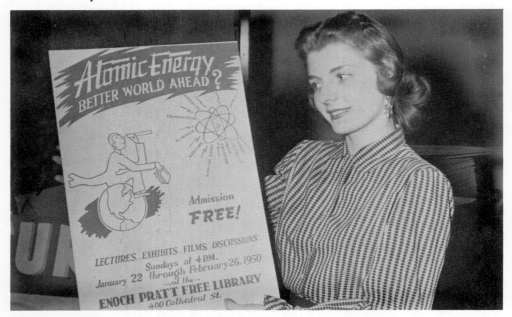

POSTER PROMOTION *Posters produced in quantity are valuable for spreading the word about the library's more ambitious shows. Recommended sizes are 9 x 12 inches, 14 x 20 inches and 17 x 22 inches, depending upon individual preference. However, the larger posters are sometimes difficult to place because of space considerations.*

Items for store windows and counter display should have cardboard easels attached. Boy Scouts and other youth groups are often willing to deliver the posters, but the original contacts should be made by the librarian.

62

Letters calling attention to the event may be directed to the presidents of organizations for announcement at meetings, and book marks or fliers may be distributed from supermarkets, shopping centers, banks, skating rinks, and other places frequented by large numbers of people.

Information intended for radio and television, short and to the point, should reach program directors two weeks or ten days before the exhibit starts. At the Enoch Pratt Free Library it is the practice to send a group of spot announcements, ranging in length from 25 to 125 words, to all local stations. These can be used in breaks between programs at any hour of the day or night, and are difficult for listeners to escape. Therefore, they are more effective than ordinary full-length library programs, which have a limited audience and are up against stiff commercial competition.

(Of course, it is also desirable whenever possible for the librarian to make guest appearances on well-established, popular programs. In this way the exhibits message can be additionally projected.)

If there is no early display deadline set, preface each spot announcement with the line: **SPOT ANNOUNCEMENT FOR ANY CONVENIENT TIME.**

When a given period for broadcasting is desired, specify it: **SPOT ANNOUNCEMENT FOR JUNE 18, 19 AND 20, 19....**

Type and capitalize all copy, double or triple-space, using plain white paper, 8½ x 11 inches, one side only. In the upper left-hand corner note your name, library address and telephone number, for quick identification and reference.

Learn the wishes of your local stations. Some prefer original copies of individual "spots" on separate sheets of paper. Others will take several announcements on a single sheet, originals or carbons. It goes without saying that all carbon copies must be distinct and legible. When composing the "spots," vary your phraseology, even though repeating the basic information.

Following are a few radio and television examples associated with Baltimore exhibits projects in past years:

SPOT ANNOUNCEMENT FOR ANY CONVENIENT TIME, NOVEMBER 20 — DECEMBER 22.

IT'S CHRISTMAS FAIRYLAND TIME AT THE ENOCH PRATT FREE LIBRARY. ENJOY THE DELIGHTFUL CHRISTMAS BOOK SHOW AT THE LIBRARY'S MAIN BUILDING, DAILY EXCEPT SUNDAY, THROUGH DECEMBER 26.

SPOT ANNOUNCEMENT FOR WEDNESDAY, THURSDAY, FRIDAY, SATURDAY (NOVEMBER 14, 15, 16, 17)

HAVE YOU A BOOK GIFT PROBLEM? THEN BE SURE TO VISIT THE ENOCH PRATT FREE LIBRARY'S CHRISTMAS BOOK SHOW, OPENING MONDAY AT THE LIBRARY'S MAIN BUILDING, 400 CATHEDRAL STREET. IN GAY CARNIVAL ATMOSPHERE YOU MAY LOOK OVER BOOKS FOR ALL AGES AND READING TASTES — BOOKS TO SUIT EVERY PURSE AND PURPOSE.

SPOT ANNOUNCEMENT FOR WEDNESDAY, THURSDAY, FRIDAY, SATURDAY (NOVEMBER 14, 15, 16, 17)

DON'T MISS THE ENOCH PRATT FREE LIBRARY'S CHRISTMAS BOOK SHOW, STARTING MONDAY AT THE MAIN BUILDING, CATHEDRAL AND FRANKLIN STREETS. ENJOY THE JOLLY SANTA CLAUS DECORATIONS, THE COLORFUL BOOK BOOTHS, AND OTHER ATTRACTIVE FEATURES. LET TRAINED SPECIALISTS SOLVE YOUR PERSONAL BOOK GIFT PROBLEMS. THE PRATT LIBRARY'S CHRISTMAS BOOK SHOW WILL BE OPEN FROM 9 A.M. TO 9 P.M. DAILY EXCEPT SUNDAYS AND HOLIDAYS THROUGH DECEMBER 26.

SPOT ANNOUNCEMENT FOR USE NOW THROUGH MARCH 24.

IMPORTANT BOOKS OF THE TWENTIETH CENTURY, INCLUDING THE FAVORITES OF PROMINENT BALTIMOREANS, WILL GO ON DISPLAY TUESDAY, MARCH 25 IN THE PRATT LIBRARY. HOW MANY HAVE YOU READ? HOW MANY HAVE YOU MISSED? VISIT THE PRATT'S CENTRAL BUILDING AND RENEW ACQUAINTANCE WITH THESE BOOKS WHICH ARE PART OF AMERICA'S HERITAGE.

SPOT ANNOUNCEMENT FOR USE MARCH 25 AND AFTER

MEMORABLE YEARS — 1901 to 1950! YEARS OF WAR AND PEACE, BREADLINES, BOOMS AND STARTLING HEADLINES. WHAT BOOKS HAVE AMERICANS READ DURING THESE EVENTFUL TIMES? VISIT THE PRATT LIBRARY'S EXHIBITION OF NOTABLE BOOKS OF THE LAST HALF-CENTURY, AND SEE FOR YOURSELF. THE SHOW WILL REMAIN THROUGH MAY 17. LIBRARY HOURS ARE 9 A.M. TO 9 P.M. DAILY EXCEPT SUNDAY.

SPOT ANNOUNCEMENT FOR USE MARCH 25 AND AFTER

REMEMBER WHEN F. SCOTT FITZGERALD WAS THE RAGE AND SINCLAIR LEWIS'S "MAIN STREET" CAUSED A FUROR? THE TWENTIETH CENTURY IS RICH IN MEMORABLE BOOKS AND THE ENOCH PRATT FREE LIBRARY NOW HAS ON DISPLAY A SPECIAL EXHIBIT OF BOOKS OF THE HALF CENTURY FROM 1901 to 1950. BE SURE TO SEE IT. ENJOY SOME OF THE FAMOUS TITLES OF THOSE TIMES.

CHAPTER NINE

BASIC SILK SCREEN

When a library bond issue or some other major project requiring all-out publicity is pending, the silk screen process is excellent for producing display posters and signs in quantity for community-wide distribution.

Conducted somewhat on the printing press principle, but operated manually by small, noncommercial agencies, the silk screen is both time and labor-saving, particularly for medium-sized and larger libraries with the necessary staff.

Essential equipment and materials are as follows:

Silk screen film
Film-stencil knife
Clear gummed tape
Masking tape
12 XX silk screen stencil silk, meshes 124 per inch
Adhering solution
Silk screen paint solvent
Lacquer thinner
Silk screen paints
Squeegee
¼ inch plywood

Glue
Metal hinges (two)
Stapling gun with staples
Cardboard (or paper) of desired thickness
Brown wrapping paper
Work table or bench
White cloths
Printing frame (or four 2 x 4's)

SILK SCREEN FRAME *This frame, or box, is large enough to take a full sheet of cardboard, 28 x 44 inches. Because of its size, making hand-manipulation of long runs tiring, a pulley device was attached, to help carry the weight during the raising and lowering process. Pulley ropes have here been temporarily disconnected. Note the "window" with film design on the silk exposed, ready to receive the paint.*

65

A simple silk screen printing frame or box can be purchased or made inexpensively. To build one, determine the largest size poster or sign you are likely to need in quantity, and allow a four-inch margin all around. Accordingly, if your biggest poster is to be 22 by 28 inches, saw two 2 by 4's to a length of 26 inches, and another pair to a length of 32 inches. Nail the pieces together or, better still, groove the joints, gluing the edges. The latter method is preferable, because the frame must be rigid in construction for precise registry.

Lay the silk on the frame, with the edges overlapping; stretch at both ends and staple overhanging edges tightly all around, so there are no sags or distortions. When this is done wet the silk thoroughly, then let dry. This draws the silk taut, as it must be, for satisfactory performance. Next cover the stapled areas and sides of the box with several layers of two-inch masking tape, to keep them smooth and neat. The frame is now finished.

Set a piece of quarter-inch plywood a few inches larger than the frame on a rough table or bench, the front edges parallel, and nail the plywood on its face. Then with two sturdy metal hinges attach the box securely to the rear section of the plywood. This will keep it in place and give accurate register.

Regardless of the color chosen for any single-paint job to be reproduced, the original pattern should be black on white, which is easiest to see under the film.

Let us say that the projected poster will measure 17 x 22 inches.

Silk screen film is a lacquer film made of two layers (the bottom layer is a supporting sheet of wax paper) manufactured in rolls 300 by 40 inches, or it may be purchased by the yard. Cut a piece 19 x 24 inches for the job at hand, and place over the poster pattern lacquer side up. The lettering and design are plainly visible.

Using the stencil knife, trace lightly along the outline of letters and art work with just enough pressure to cut upper surface, then peel off the portions of the lacquer film encompassed. Be careful not to damage the paper beneath. When the cutting is complete, the job is ready to apply to the silk. This is the most difficult part of the operation, and success hinges on how it comes out.

CUTTING THE STENCIL

The sharp point of the stencil knife moves lightly along the outline of the letters and illustrations on the pattern below. This is a delicate operation, and just enough pressure should be used to pierce the upper surface, without damage to the wax paper base. Then the lacquer film within the cut area is peeled off, after which the job is ready to apply to the silk.

Proceed with caution. Take the sample poster (over which the film was cut) and with four small pieces of gummed transparent tape at corners affix it to the plywood board under the frame. Then place the film over the poster so that the cutout letters and design are superimposed exactly over the original work, and tape this at corners. Avoid excessive use of tape, as too much may tear the fabric later.

Lower the box or frame, resting it on the plywood base, in preparation for transferring the pattern to the silk. Take two good-sized pieces of clean white cloth, one for applying the adhering solution and the other for wiping dry. (The adhering solution, packaged in metal cans, is highly inflammable. Be sure to enforce NO SMOKING regulations not only during the operation, but also until the leftovers are safely disposed of.)

Saturate one cloth, squeezing off the excess liquid. With that in one hand and the dry cloth in the other, you are ready to begin. Take the wet cloth and with long, sweeping strokes, moisten the entire film area. As soon as this has been accomplished, repeat the action with the dry cloth. This is important, as the adhering solution dissolves the film into the silk.

An excess of wetness will make the penetration too deep, ruining the stencil. On the other hand, if the cloth is not wet enough, the film will not adhere properly to the silk, and the results will be disappointing. If possible, experiment with a few small pieces of film in advance, until the proper technique is mastered.

When the film has adhered to the silk, let it dry for about five minutes. The adhering liquid evaporates very quickly. During this time raise the frame, and with a pencil draw two lines along the left side and top of the sample poster. Then take two narrow cardboard strips and lay them against the pencil lines, facing out. Tape, tack or staple them carefully into position. The angle-like arrangement will serve as guide lines.

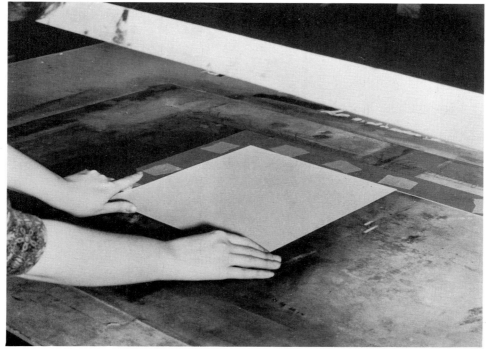

INSERTING THE POSTER BOARD   *Top and left edges must be placed flush against the cardboard guideline strips for exact registry, otherwise the printing will be off balance. Speed is imperative, as silk screen paints dry rapidly. As each poster is imprinted it is withdrawn and a new card slipped into position, without waste of time or motion.*

By this time the film should be dry. Peel off the wax paper backing. If the film has adhered properly, the paper will strip off cleanly. Should any part of the film be removed with the paper, replace the latter, drop the box, and with the damp cloth rub the part in question lightly until it has adhered, then remove the paper entirely.

At this point take a piece of brown wrapping paper slightly larger than the box. Cut from it a section extending just a little beyond the film area, then affix the paper to the frame with only the cut-out or "window" section of the silk exposed.

Attach the brown paper to the sides of the box with short strips of masking tape, and use a double thickness of the tape around the edge of the "window" opening. Make sure the tape is down tight and smooth, so that no paint can seep through. The screen is then ready to run.

The correct number of poster cards, all measured meticulously and of uniform size, should be at hand on a nearby table or book truck, where they may be picked up quickly, one by one. It is wise to have a few more than the number needed, as insurance against spoilage. Commercial houses generally allow 10 per cent for poor impressions, but the Enoch Pratt Free Library seldom has more than one or two to a job, even when hundreds of copies are involved.

For the "dry run," or preliminary testing, the Pratt uses old newspaper pages. In that way, if an imperfection appears, it can be corrected without waste of cardboard.

Silk screen paints are obtainable in a variety of colors, but the supplier will provide instructions for mixing special shades when desired. Stir paint well. If too thick, add silk screen

OPERATION SQUEEGEE

A small quantity of silk screen paint of the desired color is poured from the can to the right of the "window," the full length of the film. Then the exhibits worker, holding the wooden handle of the squeegee, with the rubber blade pushes the paint firmly across the film. This transfers the pattern to the card below.

"CLOTHESLINE" DRYERS *Overhead wires strung from wall to wall, with metal clips attached, can accommodate a large run of freshly silkscreened items without cluttering regular work space.*

paint solvent. The solvent is used also for cleaning up the paint after the job is done, and lacquer thinner removes the stencil from silk.

When paint is at proper consistency, make sure that the first card is in the correct position under the frame, inserted against the guideline strips. Place newspaper over this, and lower frame. Pour a small quantity of paint from the can to the right of the "window," the full length of the film. Next take the squeegee (the tool which forces the paint through the silk) and, holding the wooden handle, push the rubber blade firmly across the film. Raise the box, remove the newspaper, and check to see that the paint has come through evenly, giving the letters and illustration a sharp, clean line.

If all is well begin to run the cards, squeegeeing paint back and forth, raising and lowering frame as required, removing screened card each time and placing a fresh card in position until the work is completed. Add more paint as needed. If the letters are light and not fully coated at times, the paint is too thick. Conversely, if paint spreads too fast, it is too thin.

Imprinted cards, when wet, can be stacked standing around the room to dry. The Pratt Library has three long overhead wires strung like clotheslines, wall to wall in the Exhibits Workoom, with metal clips attached. This allows suspension of several hundred posters or signs simultaneously, without cluttering up the regular work space. For best results silk screen items should dry overnight.

SILK SCREEN STACKING *When no drying racks are available, posters may be placed against each other in the manner of building a house of cards. However, care must be exercised, or the whole arrangement will collapse.*

If the budget permits, multicolor jobs can be produced. Cut a separate film for each color. Before starting a new run make sure the cleanup of the preceding run has been thorough, and the register properly adjusted. The printing register must be perfect every time, as overlapping or inaccurate placement will ruin the work. Whenever possible do silk screening in dry weather, as dampness may add to operational difficulties.

NOTE: For special problems and advice, consult your graphic arts supplier.

DIVERSIFIED DISPLAY SUGGESTIONS

*Library exhibits may relate to any idea or subject tying
in with materials in the library's collection.*

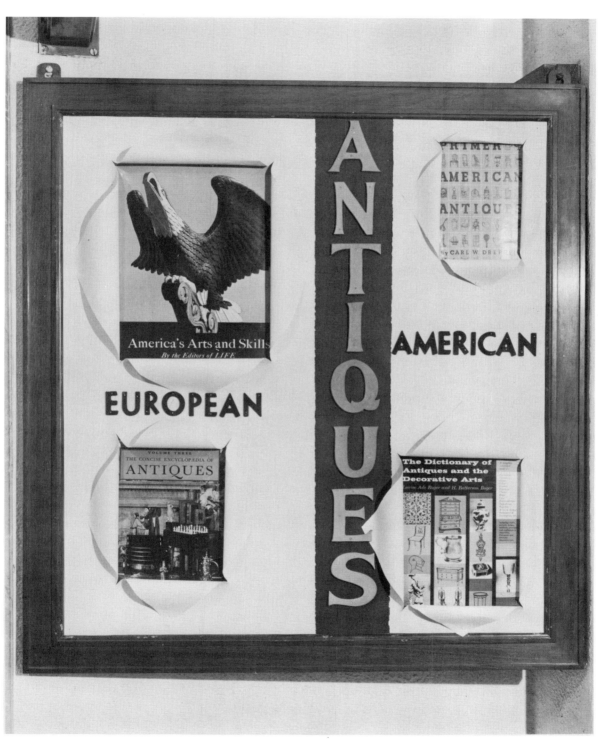

A SIMPLE BULLETIN BOARD *With book jackets projected from paper "windows." Prepared by the Enoch Pratt Free Library's Fine Arts Department.*

74

RE-USING MATERIAL *As these photographs indicate, display decorations may be repeated if the arrangement varies. The backdrop illustrations were cut from travel posters which had outlived their usefulness.*

COLORFUL CUTOUTS

The figurines shown were originally part of a travel poster. They were salvaged when the poster edges became tattered.

TREATMENT CAN BE VARIED

While subjects may be repeated from time to time, the displays should be handled differently. The illustrations on both backdrops presented here are commercial poster cutouts.

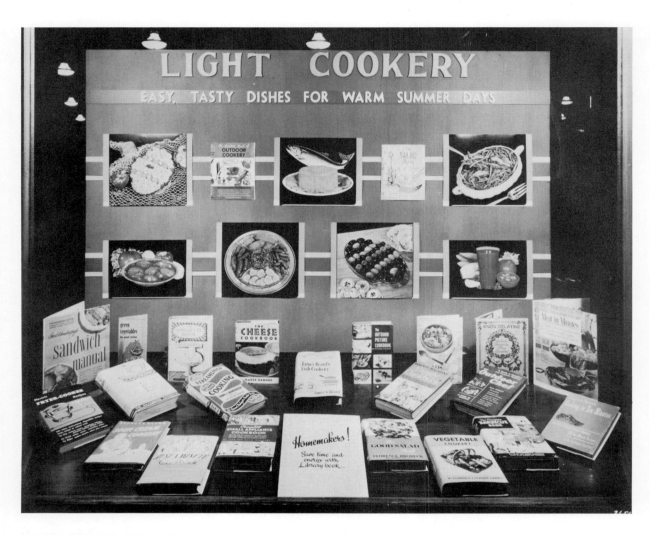

DELICATESSEN STORE DONATIONS *These tempting food pictures were obtained free through the good offices of a dealer in cooked meats, pickles, preserves and relishes.*

VOTE — THE BALLOT IS THE LIFEBLOOD OF DEMOCRACY

NATIONAL NEWSPAPER WEEK

THE NEWBERY - CALDECOTT MEDALS

ALL ABOUT THE WEATHER

NOTES ON NATURE

SEED CATALOG TIME

PRINTING WEEK

SELF-INSTRUCTIVE PIANO BOOK

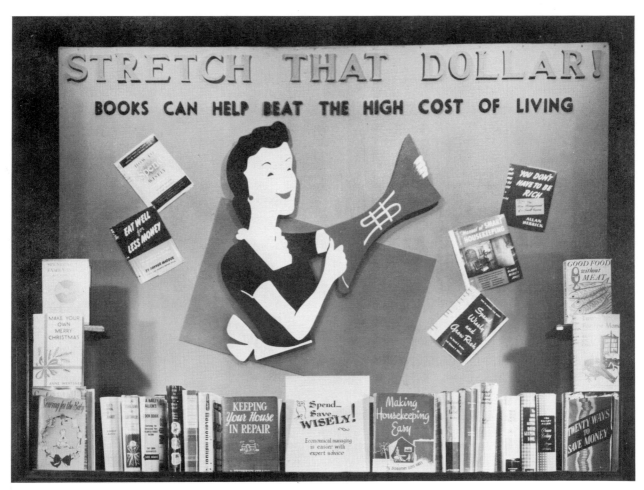

STRETCH THAT DOLLAR

ARMED FORCES WEEK

GIVE THE OLD FAVORITES

WAKE UP AND READ

MENTAL HEALTH

LENTEN READING

"DOLLS' HOUSE BALLET"

95

SUMMER SPORTS

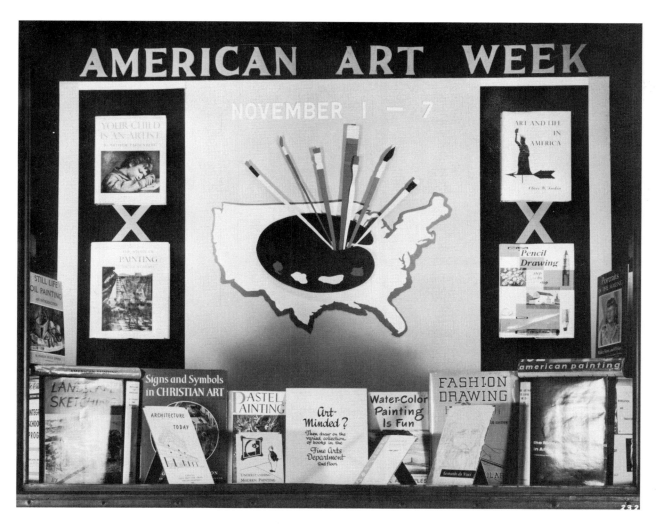

AMERICAN ART WEEK

UNITED NATIONS

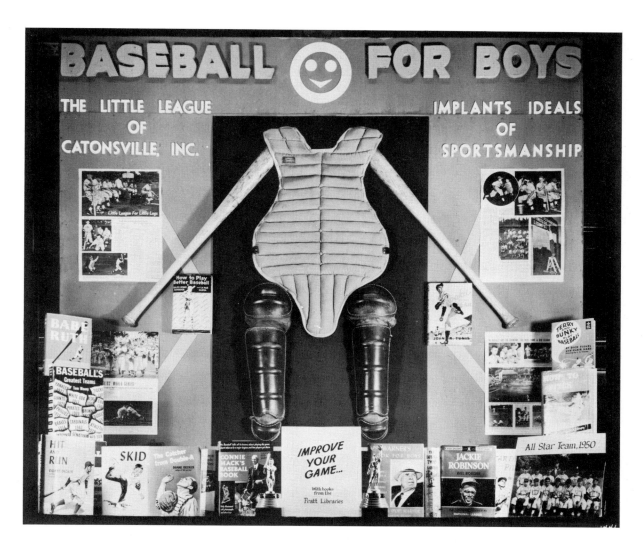

BASEBALL FOR BOYS

INTER-FAITH BASEBALL GAME

NEXT QUESTION?

BOOKS FOR A HAPPIER CHRISTMAS AND A MORE INTERESTING NEW YEAR

MAP-MINDED?

BOOKS TO GROW ON

HAPPY MOTORING

BORROWED IDEA

The eye-catching center decoration is a card-board enlargement of the magazine cover appearing to left and right.

APPENDIX

NOTE: The following pages present suggestions and information which the author hopes may prove helpful. The lists are in no sense "complete" in so far as their respective areas are concerned.

To attract attention, display "headlines" must have instantaneous appeal for readers. Brevity is desirable. Alliteration is often effective, but should not be overdone.

The main caption is designed to give a clue to the exhibit's general coverage. It is well to add a supplementary line, too, pointing up the book content. Here are a few examples from the Enoch Pratt Free Library:

MIND OVER MATTER
Human Behavior Makes Interesting Reading

TO THE LADIES!
Books That Enhance Feminine Attractiveness
and Charm

LIFE'S LIGHTER SIDE
Enjoy Some of the Library's Wit-and-Humor
Volumes

PERENNIAL FAVORITES
Books That Have Stood the Test of Time

LONG, LONG AGO
Stories of Other Days and Ways

BOOKS FOR THE WHOLE FAMILY
Good Reading for the Longer Evenings Ahead

PLANNING A PARTY?
Assure Its Success with Library Books

WORLD COOKERY
Try a Few Dishes That Are Different,
with the Help of These Books

ARM-CHAIR TRAVEL
Tour the Country with These
Entertaining Books

STRETCH THAT DOLLAR!
Books Can Help Beat the High Cost of Living

BOOK TONIC
A Sure Cure for Spring Fever

OTHER CAPTION SUGGESTIONS:

MEET THE AUTHORS
  BOOKS FOR LAZY DAYS
    INDIAN TALES AND TRAILS
      "BLESSED EVENT" BOOKS
        BUILD YOUR BUSINESS WITH BOOKS
          BROTHERHOOD...PATTERN FOR PEACE
            THE GREAT AND NEAR-GREAT
              HERE'S HOUSING
                OUR AMERICAN HERITAGE
                  A TREASURE CHEST OF CHILDREN'S STORIES
                    ROSES ARE READ
                      KEEP ON LEARNING
                        BOOKS THAT BOYS LIKE
                          FIGHT INFLATION
                            PET PROBLEMS!
                              HAPPY MOTORING!
                                ADVENTURES IN SCIENCE
                                  COLLECTOR'S LUCK
                                    DRUG DISCOVERIES
                                      VACATION READING
                                        THE EMPLOYMENT PICTURE
                                          POINTERS ON PLASTICS

ONCE UPON A TIME...
  BIRD NEIGHBORS
    HOLIDAYS AHEAD
      READ 'EM, COWBOY
        GO PLACES WITH BOOKS
          THE MAGIC OF MAPS
            READING FOR FUN
              SPRINGTIME IS READING TIME
                HELPS FOR HOMEMAKERS
                  BOOKS IN SEARCH OF CHILDREN
                    WINTER WANDERINGS
                      CHILDREN'S ROOM "SPECIALS"
                        BOOK FARE FOR THE FOURTH
                          WEATHER OR NO...
                            TODAY'S CHILDREN
                              AMERICA'S STORY
                                CANADA BOUND — BY BOOK
                                  EXPLORERS ALL!
                                    HORSE AND BUGGY DAYS
                                      THE LAND OF MAKE-BELIEVE
                                        COOL READING FOR WARM DAYS
                                          MOUNTAIN MAGIC

If You Want to Mix Your Own Paints . . .

Red + Yellow	=	**Orange**
Yellow + Blue	=	**Green**
Blue + Red	=	**Purple**
Blue + White	=	**Lavender**
Purple + White	=	**Powder Blue**
Red + White	=	**Pink**
Black + White	=	**Grey**
Orange + Purple	=	**Brown**
Brown + White	=	**Tan**
Brown + Red	=	**Terracotta**
Orange + Red	=	**Tangerine**
Yellow + Orange	=	**Golden Yellow**
Red + Purple	=	**Turkey Red**
Black + Blue	=	**Navy Blue**
Blue + Green	=	**Turquoise**
Green + Yellow	=	**Jade Green**
Green + Small Amount Black	=	**Forest Green**

To make a color lighter add white

To make a color duller and darker add black, or:

A trace of Green will dull Red	A trace of Red will dull Green
" " Yellow " " Purple	" " Purple " " Yellow
" " Orange " " Blue	" " Blue " " Orange

NOTE: In combining paints, use small amounts at a time, and stir well after each addition.

When matching colors, it is advisable to let a small sample of the mixed paint dry thoroughly for best comparison. Tones have a tendency to lighten in the drying process.

Allied Chemical and Dye Corporation, Barrett Division

40 Rector Street
New York 6, N. Y.

(Charts, "Products Derived from Coal")

American Forest Products Industries

1816 N Street, N. W.
Washington 6, D. C.

(Charts: "Products of the Tree Farm" and "Where We Grow Our Trees")

American Seating Company

9th and Broadway
Grand Rapids 2, Mich.

(Series of Posture Posters)

Association of American Railroads, School and College Service

Dr. Thomas J. Sinclair,
Public Relations Department
Transportation Building
Washington 6, D. C.

(Posters and booklets on railroads and railroading)

Bristol-Myers Products Division, Educational Service Department

45 Rockefeller Plaza
New York 20, N. Y.

(Charts: "Dental Health" and "Personal Grooming", primarily designed as teaching aids. Teachers' requests should include name, title or position, subject and grade taught, number of girls and number of boys enrolled in class)

Denoyer-Geppert Company

5235-59 Ravenswood Avenue
Chicago 40, Ill.

(Illustrated booklets, "Toward Better Understanding and Use of Maps, Globes and Charts")

General Motors Corporation, Educational Relations Section

P. O. Box 177
Detroit 2, Mich.

("Automobile Story Kit")

Goodyear Tire and Rubber Company

Akron 16, Ohio

(Poster, "Automobiles" — while quantity lasts)

Manufacturing Chemists' Association, Inc.

1625 Eye Street, N. W.
Washington 6, D. C.

(Charts: "Big Question of Science" and "What Science Means to You". Only one copy of each supplied free of charge to a school. Additional copies 15¢ each)

National Audubon Society

1130 Fifth Avenue
New York 28, N. Y.

(Folders and catalogs)

National Foot Health Council

P. O. Box 57
Rockland, Mass.

(Four posters on foot care)

National Safety Council

425 N. Michigan Avenue
Chicago 11, Ill.

(Single copies of posters and pamphlets, as samples)

Revere Copper & Brass, Inc.

288 Park Avenue
New York 17, N. Y.

(A set of colored pictures on Paul Revere)

Sonotone Corporation

Elmsford, N. Y.

(Charts: "How We Hear" and "Sectional Diagram of the Human Ear". Pamphlet: "Mechanical Principles of the Human Ear")

Telephone Company (Local Business Office)

(Booklets: "The Magic of Communication," "The Story of Alexander Graham Bell" and others)

U. S. Projects Officer

718 Jackson Place
Washington 6, D. C.

(Maps and charts relating to the Antarctic)

POSSIBLE SOURCES OF FREE TRAVEL

POSTERS, FOLDERS AND/OR BOOKLETS

American Airlines
  100 Park Avenue
  New York, N. Y.
American Express Company
  65 Broadway
  New York 6, N. Y.
      (Contact local office first, if one is available)
Atchison, Topeka and Santa Fe
  Railroad Company
    1416-18 Philadelphia National
      Bank Building
    Philadelphia, Pa.
British Information Service
  30 Rockefeller Plaza
  New York 20, N. Y.
British-Columbia Government Travel Bureau
  Department of Trade and Industry
    Victoria
    British Columbia, Canada
British Travel and Holidays Association
  336 Madison Avenue
  New York 17, N. Y.
Canadian Government Travel Bureau
  Department of Transport
    Ottawa, Canada
Cuban Tourist Commission
  336 East Flagler Street
  Miami, Fla.
Canadian National Railways
  922 15th Street, N. W.
  Washington 5, D. C.
Collins, Tom (Bermuda - Haiti)
  122 East 42nd Street
  New York 17, N. Y.
Eastern Airlines
  405 Colorado Building
  14th and G Streets, N. W.
  Washington 5, D. C.
French Cultural Services
  972 Fifth Avenue
  New York 21, N. Y.
Great Northern Railway Company
  St. Paul, Minn.
Japan Tourist Association
  1, 1 - Chome, Marunouchi
    Chiyodaku
    Tokyo, Japan
New York Central Railroad,
  Public Relations Department
    466 Lexington Avenue
    New York 17, N. Y.
New Zealand Embassy
  Washington 8, D. C.

Northern Pacific Railway Company,
  Advertising and Publicity
    St. Paul 1, Minn.
Norwegian National Travel Office
  290 Madison Avenue
  New York 17, N. Y.
Pan American World Airways
  135 East 42nd Street
  New York 17, N. Y.
Pennsylvania Railroad Company
  Transportation Center
  6 Penn Center Plaza
  Philadelphia 4, Pa.
Publicity Bureau,
  Department of Economic Affairs
    Edmonton
    Alberta, Canada
Puerto Rican Government,
  Division of Tourism
    Economic Development Commission
    579 Fifth Avenue
    New York 17, N. Y.
Quebec Tourist Bureau
  106, Grand Allee
  Quebec, Canada
Southern Pacific Railway
  220 Shoreham Building
  Washington, D. C.
Spanish Tourist Bureau
  Duque de Medinaceli, 2
  Madrid, Spain
Swedish National Travel Office
  630 Fifth Avenue
  New York 20, N. Y.
Swiss National Tourist Office,
  Official Agency Swiss Federal Railways
    10 W. 49th Street at Rockefeller Plaza
    New York 20, N. Y.
Union Pacific Railroad Company,
  Advertising Department
    1416 Dodge Street
    Omaha 2, Nebraska
Victoria and Island Publicity Bureau
  P. O. Box 1000
  Victoria, British Columbia
  Canada
Western Air Lines
  6060 Avion Drive
  Los Angeles 45, California
Western Canadian Greyhound Lines,
  Travel Bureau
    Greyhound Building
    Calgary
    Canada

American Institute of Baking
  400 East Ontario Street
  Chicago 11, Ill.

   (Nutrition charts and guides)

American Telephone and Telegraph Company
  195 Broadway
  New York 7, N. Y.

   (Posters)

Automobile Manufacturing Association
  New Center Building
  Detroit 2, Mich.

   (Posters, pamphlets)

General Mills, Inc.
  Department of Public Service
  400 Second Avenue, South
  Minneapolis, Minn.

   (Pamphlets and folders on nutrition)

General Motors Corporation,
  Executive Offices,
  Electro-Motive Division
  Le Grange, Ill.

   (Posters of different railroads in the United States)

New York Department of Commerce
  112 State Street
  Albany 7, N. Y.

   (Posters)

Pan-American Coffee Bureau
  120 Wall Street
  New York 5, N. Y.

   (Picture maps relating to the growth, production and distribution of coffee)

Sunkist Growers
  226 West Ontario Street
  Chicago 10, Ill.

   (Posters of citrus fruits)

U. S. Department of Agriculture,
  A. R. S. Information
  Washington 25, D. C.
   (Posters and pamphlets on nutrition)

U. S. Department of Health, Education and Welfare
  Washington 25, D. C.
   (Posters and leaflets relating to health)

U. S. Department of Labor, Women's Bureau
  Washington 25, D. C.
   (Assorted folders and pamphlets)

SOURCES OF DISPLAYS AT RELATIVELY LOW COST

(Write for complete listings and catalogs)

The American Institute of Graphic Arts
  5 East 40th Street
  New York 16, N. Y.
   ("Fifty Books of the Year," "Children's Book Show," "Annual Textbook Show," "Design and Printing for Commerce," and others)

Mrs. John A. Pope, Chief
  Travel Exhibition Service
  Smithsonian Institution
  Washington 25, D. C.
   ("A World of Children's Books," "Art Books from Italy," "The Austrian Book," "Glimpses of Switzerland," "The Way of Chinese Landscape Painting," "Books for Young Scientists," "Pup, Cub and Kitten: Common Wild Animals and Their Young" and others)

BOOK WEEK AIDS

Children's Book Council,
  Department E
  50 West 53rd Street
  New York 19, N. Y.
   (Free brochure, "Aids for Celebrating Book Week," and calendar, which librarians and teachers must request on official stationery. Posters, streamers and booklets available, but small charge for these is made)

Mentioned here are items used by or known to the Enoch Pratt Free Library's Exhibits Division. Readers familiar with others may wish to expand the list. Those who have no access to materials in local graphic arts shops or stationery stores, may write for samples and prices of such items, if they feel so disposed, to the Becker Sign Supply Company, 321 N. Paca Street, Baltimore 1, Maryland.

Acetate Sheets

(Clear, transparent composition, .005 thick. Can be cut into strips ½″ wide, the ends secured together with OK clips and the loop thus formed used to hold open books or pamphlets without obscuring illustrations or printed matter. Available in 20″ x 50″ sheets)

> **Hubbs and Corning Company**
> **404 S. Eutaw Street**
> **Baltimore 1, Maryland**

(Or by the yard, 40″ wide)

> **Becker Sign Supply Company**
> **321 N. Paca Street**
> **Baltimore 1, Maryland**

Adhering Solution

> **Graphic arts supplier**

Art Gum

> **Graphic arts supplier or stationery store**

Beaverboard

(Pressed paper wall board about ¼″ thick. Used as base for cutting decorations, as well as for caption letters. Smooth surface. May be purchased in sheets 4′ x 8′ and up)

> **Lumber companies**

Book racks (Wrought iron)

> **Demco Library Supplies**
> **New Haven 2, Conn.**

Book-saver (Liquid plastic)

> **Delkote, Inc.**
> **Wilmington, Del., or Berkeley, Calif.**

Cardboard

(22″ x 28″, 6-ply, for small posters)

> **Mudge Paper Company**
> **501 Water Street**
> **Baltimore 2, Maryland**

(28″ x 44″, 14-ply, for large posters, decoration and showcards)

> **Becker Sign Supply Company**
> **321 N. Paca Street**
> **Baltimore 1, Maryland**

Cardboard cutter (Jacques Shear)

> **Hobbs Manufacturing Company**
> **Worcester, Mass.**

Cases (Glass, portable)

> **Michaels Art Bronze Company**
> **231-243 Court Avenue**
> **Covington, Ky.**
> **Remington Rand**
> **315 Fourth Avenue**
> **New York 10, N. Y.**
> **John E. Sjörström Company**
> **1717 N. 10th Street**
> **Philadelphia 22, Pa.**

Cellophane (Clear, amber, other colors)

> **Graphic arts supplier**

Cloth

(Swede finish, for covering tables and other display surfaces, 54″ wide)

> **Becker Sign Supply Company**
> **321 N. Paca Street**
> **Baltimore 1, Maryland**

Cutawl Machine

> **International Register Company**
> **2620 West Washington Boulevard**
> **Chicago 12, Ill.**

Display Units

> **Design and Production, Inc.**
> **1912 Duke Street**
> **Alexandria, Va.**

Film (Silk screen)

> **Graphic arts supplier**

Film-Stencil Knife

> **Graphic arts supplier**

Gem Clips

> **Stationery store or graphic arts supplier**

Glue

(Furniture, for silk screen frame)

> **Hardware store**

Hinges (Metal)

> **Hardware store**

Inks (Lettering)

> **Graphic arts supplier**

Insulite

(Wood pulp wall board, in burlap or smooth finish. May be purchased in sheets 4' x 8' or larger)

Lumber yard or mill

Lacquer Thinner

Graphic arts supplier

Lettering Guide

Wrico Lettering Stencil
Wood-Regan Instrument Company, Inc.
184 Franklin Avenue
Nutley, N. J.

Letters

(Cutout. Write for catalogs and price lists)

Artype, Inc.
Barrington, Ill.
Becker Sign Supply Company
321 N. Paca Street
Baltimore 1, Maryland
Gaylord Bros., Inc.
155 Gifford Street
Syracuse, N. Y. or 29 N. Aurora
Street, Stockton, Calif.
Hallcraft Products Company
2930 N. Eleventh Street
Philadelphia 33, Pa.
The Holes Webway Company
St. Cloud, Minn.
Mitten's Display Letters
2 West 46th Street
New York 36, N. Y.
Mutual Aids
1946 Hillhurst Avenue
Los Angeles 27, Calif.
Redicut Letter Company
6519 West Boulevard
Inglewood, Calif.
W. L. Stensgaard and Associates, Inc.
346 N. Justine Street
Chicago 7, Ill.
The Stik-A-Letter Company
Rt. 2 — Box 286
Escondido, Calif.
"Stickee" Plastic Letters and Numbers
Arthur Goodwin and Company
2524 Brookfield Avenue
Baltimore 17, Maryland
The Tablet and Ticket Company
115 East 23rd Street
New York 10, N. Y.

OK Clips

Stationery store

Paints

(Cold water — Iddings, Mural-Tone, Pres-Kote, etc. Manufactured in paste form and mixed with water by user — approximately one pint water to quart of paste. Variety of colors)

Graphic arts supplier, or hardware store

Paints (Poster)

Graphic arts supplier

Paints (Silk screen)

Graphic arts supplier

Paper

(Brown, gummed, for the backs of cardboard decorations, to join pieces together)

Industrial Paper Company
2427 W. Baltimore Street
Baltimore 23, Maryland

Paper

(Brown, wrapping, for patterns. Roll, 36" width, 50 lb. weight)

Henry D. Mentzel and Company, Inc.
104 S. Charles Street
Baltimore 1, Maryland
Matthew C. Fenton, Inc.
514 S. Eutaw Street
Baltimore 1, Maryland
Industrial Paper Company
2427 W. Baltimore Street
Baltimore 23, Maryland

Peg Board

Demco Library Supplies
New Haven 2, Conn.

Pins

Graphic arts supplier or stationery store

Plywood

Lumber company

Projector (Enlarging)

Beseler Visual Products Company, Inc.
210 East 23rd Street
New York, N. Y.

Rubber Cement

Graphic arts supplier

Sign Machines (Very expensive)

Line-O-Scribe
Morgan Sign Machine Company
4510 N. Ravenswood Avenue
Chicago 40, Ill.
Printasign
Reynolds Printasign Company
9830 San Fernando Road
Pacoima, Calif.
Showcard Machine
Showcard Machine Company
1456 Merchandise Mart
Chicago 54, Ill.

Silk Screen Printing Frame

Graphic arts supplier

Silk Screen Stencil Silk

12xx, meshes 124 per inch)
Graphic arts supplier

Solvent (Silk screen paint)

Graphic arts supplier

Squeegee

Graphic arts supplier

Stapling Gun, Staples

Graphic arts supplier or stationery store

Tables (6', folding)

Mitchell Folda-Leg Tables
Walcott and Taylor
Mills Building
Washington, D. C.

Tacks (Thumb - white, black and colors)

Five-and-dime store, graphic arts supplier or stationery store

Tacks (Upholstery)

Hardware store

Tape (Adhesive, clear)

Stationery store or graphic arts supplier

Tape (Cloth, adhesive)

Fastape
Demco Library Supplies
Madison 1, Wis., or New Haven 2, Conn.

Tape

(Cotton, various widths, white and colors, in spools of 1,000 yards each. Useful for tying books open, and attaching books to display backdrops)
Wick Narrow Fabric Company
112 N. Twelfth Street
Philadelphia, Pa.

Tape (Masking)

Graphic arts supplier

SOME RELATED READINGS
BOOKS

Bernard, Frank J.
Dynamic Display

Eckersley, Tom
Poster Design

Griffis, Martha Hughes
How to Make Shapes in Space

Hazeltine, Mary E.
Anniversaries and Holidays

Johnson, Pauline
Creating with Paper

Lane, Janet and Tolleris, Beatrice K.
Planning Your Exhibit

Schoenoff, Herbert A. and Kurt R., and Cavanaugh, Hilda
Poster Making in the Elementary School

Zahn, Bert
Screen Process Methods of Reproduction

BOOKLETS, ARTICLES

Alexander, M. L.
Display Problem
Wilson Lib Bul 26:553 Mr '52

Book Fairs through the Year
Lib J 78:1982 N 15 '53

Bullock, A.
Special Exhibits Enliven Book Fair
ALA Bul 51:807-8 N '57

Cantwell, C. and Klesh, C. B.
Book Fairs Mean Good Merchandising for Libraries
Wilson Lib Bul 31:628-9 Ap '57

Chapin, B.
Books for Every Town
Wilson Lib Bul 26:824-6 Je '52

Dalton, S. M.
Let the Dime Store Help!
Wilson Lib Bul 25:521 Mr '51

Duchac, K. F.
Decatur Tries a Book Fair
Ill Lib 34:31-4 F '52

Emerson, M. C.
Bulletin Board Fever
Lib J 79:184-5 F 1 '54

Emerson, M. C.
Variety A-Plenty in Displays
La Lib Assn Bul 17:54-5 Spring '54

Gennaro, R. M. de
Recipes for Bulletin Board Dressing
Wilson Lib Bul 23:525+ Mr '49

Glass, M. M.
Bulletin Boards around the Calendar
Wilson Lib Bul 28:584+ Mr '54

Hall, E.
Book Exhibits on a Shoestring
Lib J 81:750-1 Jr Lib 2:14-15 Mr 15, '56
Ideas for Displays
Top News 11:22 D '54

Jones, P.
St. Paul Spring Fair
Wilson Lib Bul 30:164+ 0 '55

Lowry, W. H. and Paine, C. S.
Be an Exhibitionist
Lib J 81:2511-2513 N 1 '56

McFadden, Dorothy L.
How to Run a Book Fair
Children's Book Council

McGregor, D.
To Make Exhibits Effective
Lib J 80:469-71 Jr Lib 1:1 F 15 '55

McGuire, Alice Brooks
Through the Exhibit Window
Lib J 8:206 Jr Lib 2:2 Ja 15 '56

Neal, Mrs. F.
Cooperative Book Fairs in Arkansas
PLD Reporter 5:52-3 N '56

Peikert, C. H.
Cue for Good Bulletin Boards
Ill Lib 33:45-7 Ja '51

Pettit, F.
Improving and Coordinating Signs, Displays and Bulletin Boards
Wilson Lib Bul 26:553-5 Mr '52

Reaum, C. E.
Making Mobiles
Wilson Lib Bul 28:580-2 Mr '54

Sanborn, H. J.
Let's Look Behind the Exhibition
Lib J 74:169-73 F 1 '49

Schulze, M. E.
P.T.A. Sponsors Book Fair
Lib J 78:1988-9 N 15 '53

Stein, J. W.
Tennessee Festival
Lib J 80:1294-7 Je 1 '55

They'll Judge Your Library by Exhibits,
Take Time to Make Good Ones
Lib J 81:205 Jr Lib 2:1 Ja 15 '56

Tobey, M. E.
Do-It-Youself Library Exhibit
Lib J 79:1563-4 S 15 '54

Tompkins, Lucy
Where to Get Books for Fairs and Exhibits
Lib J 79:1644-9 Jr Lib 1:40-5 S 15 '54

Walker, R. S.
Theory of Library Display
Lib Assn Rec 58:1-6 Ja '56

Wilkes, R. C.
School Librarian Turns to Bulletin Boards
Ill Lib 35:90-2 F '53

Woodward, J. L.
School Library Bulletin Board
Wilson Lib Bul 27:540-4 Mr '53

ABBREVIATIONS

ALA Bul
American Library Association Bulletin

Ill Lib
Illinois Libraries

Lib J
Library Journal

Lib Assn Rec
Library Association Record

La Lib Assn Bul
Louisiana Library Association Bulletin

PLD Reporter
Public Libraries Division Reporter

Top News
Top of the News

Wilson Lib Bul
Wilson Library Bulletin

CALENDAR NOTES

CALENDAR NOTES

CALENDAR NOTES

CALENDAR NOTES

CALENDAR NOTES

Designed by Leo Martin